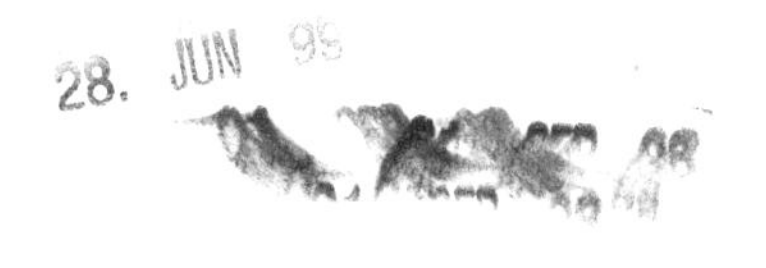

28. JUN 95

The PAPER CHASE

Also by Ivan Fallon

De Lorean:

The Rise and Fall of a Dream Maker

The Brothers:

The Rise and Fall of Saatchi and Saatchi

Billionaire:

The Life and Times of Sir James Goldsmith

The PAPER CHASE

IVAN FALLON

A Decade of Change at the DSS

HarperCollins*Publishers*

HarperCollins*Publishers*
77-85 Fulham Palace Road,
Hammersmith, London W6 8JB

Published by HarperCollins*Publishers* in
association with Andersen Consulting1993

9 8 7 6 5 4 3 2 1

Design: Bev Speight

Project Editor: Liz Dean

Illustrations: David Wood

A catalogue record for this book is available
from the British Library

ISBN 000 255244-2

Printed in Great Britain by Butler & Tanner,
Frome, Somerset.

CONTENTS

ILLUSTRATIONS

(Between pages 114 & 115)

* From Social Security Departmental Report (Cm 2213): The Government's expenditure plans 1993–94 to 1995–96.

† From Social Security Departmental Report: The Government's expenditure plans 1978–79.

FOREWORD

The idea for this book originated with Keith Burgess, managing partner of Andersen Consulting, who devoted a great deal of his time and effort to the DSS's monumental project, the Operational Strategy, and felt strongly the story of its huge achievement against the odds should not go untold. It was he who persuaded me to tell the tale of an operation which was so large and so complex that even he and his Andersen colleagues had only a hazy idea of what they were taking on – as indeed did I when I started out to write about it. Burgess and his partner Mark Otway spent many hours with me reliving its excitement, problems and eventual success, the tension when it was going badly but the joy when it worked as they intended it to. I have to thank them in particular. I also want to thank their Andersen colleagues, Dave Clinton, Al Donald, Ian Watmore, David Finn and Philippa Reid for the time they gave me. This book is a tribute to the achievements of them and the other Andersen people who put so much of themselves into the Operational Strategy. My thanks also to Sarah McMahon of Andersen.

But above all, this book is a tribute to the civil servants who conceived the Operational Strategy, lived through its difficult gestation period and finally saw it through to completion.

Sir Michael Partridge, Permanent Secretary of the Department of Social Security, and a key figure in the operation, provided invaluable help and counsel, as did one of his predecessors, Sir Geoffrey Otton, who was present at the outset. Norman Clarke recalled for me in great detail the germination of the whole project and John Spackman told me about the key middle period. Eric Caines brought it alive for me with his graphic descriptions of some of the lighter moments, as well as the tenser ones. Lord (John) Moore was able to fill me in on some of the higher, political aspects, which shed new light on some of the decision-making processes.

I am also grateful to Ian Stewart, Phil Dunn, John Kenworthy, Martin Bankier, Derek Chislett and Brian Hogarth for their courtesy, time and assistance.

The book could not have been done without the help of Bill Bloom, who accompanied me to Newcastle and Lytham St Annes and did much of the research, my daughters Tania and Lara and their mother Sue, who organised them all.

Ivan Fallon

PREFACE

In November 1980, eighteen months after the Thatcher Government had come to power in Britain, the Department of Health and Social Security issued a working paper entitled 'A Strategy for Social Security Operations'. At the time it attracted little attention in the outside world, but in Whitehall it came to be seen as a seminal document. It set out a vision of how the modern welfare system could cope with the demands of delivering increasingly complex benefits to a growing number of recipients, and paved the way for the biggest automation programme of social services Britain had ever seen. It also marked the beginning of the largest non-defence computerisation operation outside the United States.

Although in many ways the working paper was an imaginative and even visionary document, its language was cautious and tentative. It was launched into a climate of low morale and near despair by those who would be most affected by it: the 88,000 DHSS staff who were buried under an ever-growing avalanche of demands for State benefits which successive governments had vied with each other to introduce through the past thirty years.

It set out what was an all too familiar picture for those involved in Britain's creaking welfare system: there were now thirty-four different benefits, ten of them introduced in the previous decade, paid to 22 million people – amounting to over a billion payments a year. Some 8.6 million pensioners, 5 million people on income support, over a million unemployed, and 40 million national insurance contributors were being dealt with out of 1300 ill-equipped and shabby offices. A system, designed to provide many fewer and more simple benefits, was breaking down under the strain. There were delays, a growing crescendo of complaint which at times was turning into actual physical protest, inaccuracies in computations, and huge inefficiencies. The administrative cost too was rapidly getting out of hand: £109 million a year just to administer pensions, £280 million to pay out supplementary benefit, and another £56 million for child benefit.

But the message of the paper was not any of these things. It was designed, not as a critique or analysis of the system, but to offer a long-term answer. It was the result of several years of thinking and planning by a working party of the best brains in the Department, headed by a senior civil servant, Norman Clarke. It laid out what the Department from then on would call its Operational Strategy, a twenty-year plan to provide what at that moment the Department was signally unable to do: a user-friendly, accurate and efficient service to the millions who received one of the myriad of State benefits. The central message of the paper was the lesson senior officials had by now learnt the hard way: to achieve their objective, even to get close to it, could not be done simply by taking on yet more people. That had been the solution for three decades, and in the Thatcher years was no longer an option – even if anyone had thought it was the answer, which no one any longer did. Britain's Welfare State had to be brought into the modern world, which meant mechanisation on a grand and unprecedented scale. Without it, the nation's social security system, once regarded as among the best in the world, would face collapse.

The DHSS had actually been an early convert to computers, building massive batch-type systems at Newcastle to record national insurance contributions and handle pensions in the early 1960s. For several years these computers were at the forefront of the technological revolution, the envy of other Civil Service departments, and as up-to-date as anything in the private sector. But as the 1970s advanced, so the need to move to an entirely different system of computers – on-line systems with hundreds of terminals in local offices linked to mainframes – to cope with the rising tide of short-term benefits became obvious. Unemployment benefit, supplementary benefit, sickness benefit and so on could only be handled in this way. What the 1980 working paper did not say, but what the senior civil servants who drafted it knew all too well, was that the Department's own attempts to build such a computer network had so far proved beyond the capabilities of the civil servants.

The history of the administrative nightmare the welfare system had become by the end of the 1970s is well enough rehearsed. Demand for supplementary benefit alone – a means-tested benefit that was originally designed as a short-term help to supplement other benefits – required 38,000 people to administer it across the country. There were another 30,000 people in local, central and regional offices dealing with other benefits and contributions. The huge, sprawling office in Newcastle, handling 40 million contributors' accounts, was the biggest employer in the whole of the north-east – some 13,000 people – but it was of little help to the local offices all over Britain dealing with increasingly frustrated recipients who spent hours queuing for benefits. The rules of entitlement had become so complex that neither staff nor recipients understood them, and the guidance manual ran to two volumes and 16,000 paragraphs. All the main income-related benefits – supplementary benefit, housing benefit and family income supplement – used different measures of income and capital.

All of this was bad enough, but what was even worse was the method of delivering these millions of payments into the hands of those receiving welfare. The big-batch computer systems of Newcastle, efficient enough at recording pension contributions and at printing pension books, were far too inflexible to be much help to the demoralised staff behind the counters in the local offices. On-line computer systems were by now widely in use in banks, building societies and other institutions dealing with large numbers of customers, but they were unknown in the social security system, which in the local offices was still in the quill-pen era. 'The service for the public too often fails as the staff hunt for files in a Dickensian paper chase,' said the government Green Paper gloomily. This was no exaggeration. In the typical social security office, one civil servant despondently worked out, there were some forty-eight places where an individual's file could legitimately be held – and countless other illegitimate places. Clerks worked literally hidden under paperwork, with more being added by the week, so that finding the correct file, let alone acting on it, was a major task by itself. 'We identified in the course of a particular exercise that the same information was held on different records in 13 different places,' said Eric Caines, one of the civil servants who was to play a key role in modernising it. 'People who had a whole series of claims from child benefit to sickness benefit, supplementary benefit and so on were all on different records, and people were going around collecting the stuff again and again. The papers would often be out of the file, or they might have been sent to Newcastle in pursuit of a child benefit query, or what have you. So there was this huge paper chase, with people left waiting for interminable periods.'

Frustration on the part of both recipients and DHSS staff was building into a serious political issue, yet from 1976 onwards both Labour and Conservative governments were cutting back on administrative spending, demanding that every department – and with its huge workforce, social security was high on the target list – must reduce manpower. From well before the International Monetary Fund imposed swingeing public expenditure cuts across the board on the Labour government of the 1970s, ministers and officials were keenly aware that, without fundamental change, the system was headed for crisis.

The Department had, after its own fashion, done its best. It had tried to modernise, making several botched attempts at designing a system that would at least bring the local offices up to the levels used in the banks. Aware that the systems at Newcastle, despite their relative sophistication in processing huge bundles of claims, were too inflexible for its needs, the Department set out to create an integrated system which would be state-of-the-art. It knew what it needed: a system whereby a claimant could appear at an office anywhere in the country, identify himself to the computer (not all claimants know their social security number, so the system would have to be clever enough to help find it for them), which could then produce the information needed to process the claim rapidly, efficiently and accurately. The on-line computer would have a query facility connected to a big computer placed somewhere else containing the person's files. Paperwork would be reduced dramatically, queues shortened instantly, and the pressure taken off the overworked staff.

The theory was fine, but the practice was another matter. In the 1960s and early 1970s, there had been a number of attempts to produce an on-line system to automate several of the major benfits – supplementary benefit and incapacity benefit in particular – but the scale of the task defied the best computer brains in the Department. The most spectacular was called CAMELOT, a state-of-the-art system designed largely by systems analysts from Newcastle and the Department's other centres. Like its predecessors, it was a failure, closed in 1981 by an embarrassed DHSS which had to explain away yet another disaster to a sceptical Public Accounts Committee, the all-party House of Commons watchdog on government spending. Sir Geoffrey Otton, the Department's second permanent secretary, tried vainly to persuade the sceptical committee members that CAMELOT was only a 'failure in the sense that it was an experiment that failed', adding that it was 'unfinished business as far as I am concerned.' In fact, although it contained a number of technological breakthroughs, the CAMELOT venture would have long-term repercussions for the Department, as many of the civil servants involved with it at the time now acknowledge. It was a crippling blow to the Department's own belief in its abilities to solve its own technology problems from within.

The CAMELOT experiment, however, had another side to it. It was to provide the catalyst for some serious re-assessment. The senior officials now accepted that they could not go on processing claims on a benefit by benefit basis, but would have to work towards a system where they would have to have a complete picture of an individual's needs – his contribution record, number of children, other benefits received, and so on, all available on one computer terminal. In short, a picture of the 'whole person', at least insofar as social security was concerned, would be instantly available on a single terminal anywhere in the country.

The implications of that were considerable. It meant a complete restructuring of the way benefits were delivered, a huge refurbishment programme of over 500 offices, and a mass retraining and education programme. Because it also presented a technical challenge beyond the reach of the Department's own staff, it meant thinking the unthinkable: seeking helping from the world outside Whitehall and Newcastle. The working paper, and the collapse of CAMELOT, were eventually to bring the Department to Andersen Consulting, a firm which could boast that it was the leading consultancy in the world in the areas of information technology and integrated systems. Over the next eight years or so, the Department, with the help and advice of Andersen and other consultants, would, with many a hairy moment along the way, transform the way in which it coped with its mountain of paperwork.

Andersen was hired just before Christmas 1982 on the basis of a modest contract. Five people, working for three years, were to provide 'an independent management and technical view of progress' of the Department's Operational Strategy, as set out in that working paper. But within six months the Andersen team had grown to fifteen, and by the year-end it was forty. At the peak, it had over 250 consultants working alongside the civil servants who would eventually begin to install a system in the DSS local offices in February 1989. Along the way there would be many technical 'firsts', as Andersen advised on computerising systems containing millions of records, created the integrated OSI-based network required by the Government, a set of linked applications, a central index, four major data centres, and a common technical architecture which would provide the local offices with access to much of the different information on a single terminal. During that time, the consultants and civil servants working together on the project were continually pushing forward the frontiers of technology, finding leading-edge but practical solutions to a scale of problems not encountered before.

In an extraordinary concentrated burst of energy, the full 'roll-out' of the system was completed in just two and a half years, ending in July 1991, paving the way for even more sophisticated delivering of benefits – including much more streamlined claims and payments procedures.

By the time the immediate objectives of the Operational Strategy were completed in mid-1991, the Department had installed 40,000 user terminals feeding off seventy-two mainframe computers, which would cost in all around £1.8 billion by the year 2000. In the north-east of England, near Newcastle, a central index held the name, address and date of birth of over 50 million people, virtually the whole of the British population, accessible in seconds from anywhere in the country. An operation that was becoming so unwieldy and overloaded that ministers were being advised to hold back on further changes and new benefits was now delivering at a speed and efficiency rate it had never known before.

Yet the behind-the-scenes story of the Operational Strategy is much more dramatic than that. It involves enormous commitment on the part of the key civil servants who drove it through the minefields that lay in wait, considerable courage in tackling the culture changes needed, and determination to stand up to the strikes that threatened to shut the whole operation down. There would be opposition, fierce at times, from the entrenched trade unions, and more passively from those who felt their principalities were being threatened by the new systems. There were prejudices, personality clashes and bureaucracies to be overcome. There were massive technical problems too: computerising an operation as complex and as large as Britain's welfare system was probably not technologically possible in 1980 – although few people knew that at the time – and finding a way of doing it stretched to the limit the skills and innovativeness of some of the most experienced information technology consultants in the world. What started for Andersen as an interesting but by no means earth-shattering piece of work grew to the point where it became its biggest ever contract in Britain, with its people at the very heart of the government machine, working shoulder to shoulder with some of the leading civil servants of the day.

Above all, the story of the Operational Strategy is one of government and the private sector working together, of friendships formed and tensions and conflicts ironed out in everyday working circumstances. It is a story of senior civil servants who recognised the need for a modern system, obtained the necessary clearances from ministers, argued it through the Treasury – no mean feat in itself – and then put their hearts into making it work.

It is also a success story: at the end of the day, the system delivered much of what it was asked to, and today the senior civil servants openly admit what they never would have done a decade ago – they could not have done it without help.

CHAPTER ONE
THE LURE *of* CAMELOT

Neither civil servants nor ministers had ever needed much convincing of the advantages of computerising Britain's social security system. Probably no business in the world produced more paper and used more forms, and as the system grew in the 1950s and 1960s, so the numbers employed grew too, but never as fast as the task they were required to achieve. The surge in new benefits and in government spending on Britain's social framework was without precedent, and by today's more austere standards of growth is difficult to imagine. In 1952, when the post-Beveridge social security system was still in its infancy, Britain was spending £1.7 billion a year on it, equivalent to half the defence budget and not much more than it was spending on health. By 1968, social security spending had grown by 143% in real terms, was now twice the health budget, and was £1 billion bigger than the £3 billion spent on defence.

Against a background of high economic growth, both major political parties competed feverishly to introduce new benefits – and neither party took kindly to Treasury ministers who tried to call a halt. In 1958, when the Chancellor, Peter Thorneycroft, complained that 'we have sought to maintain a welfare state at as high a level as – sometimes even a higher level than – that of the United States', Harold Macmillan refused to accept proposals to withdraw family allowance for the second child in each family – it was at that time payable for second and subsequent children, but not the first. Thorneycroft, together with his fellow Treasury ministers Enoch Powell and Nigel Birch, resigned. In other circumstances the resignation of the whole Treasury team would have pushed a government into a serious crisis, but Thorneycroft was fighting against the mood at the time. Macmillan, in one of his most famously memorable phrases, dismissed it as just 'a little local difficulty'. Britain's welfare system went on growing.

But it could not go on for ever, simply because economists

were already gloomily forecasting that, at the exponential rates achieved through the 1950s and 1960s, by the end of the century Britain would be committing over 100% of its Gross National Product to welfare. Long before then – and the problem was apparent from the mid-1950s – the sheer logistical task of delivering the proliferation of benefits to the growing numbers who could claim them would swamp the system. Without automation and a huge increase in productivity, delivery was going to fall hopelessly behind political aspirations and promises.

The endless flow of repetitive clerical tasks made pensions in particular perfect territory for mechanisation, and in the days of full employment there was barely a whimper of protest when the first machines were installed as early as 1959. They were physically enormous and inflexible computers by later standards, but in the late 1950s and early 1960s they were state-of-the-art – and in the fledgling days of computers, when anyone with the smallest degree of knowledge stood above the rest, the people who operated them were soon regarded as superior wizards, a factor that was to lead to problems later. Because the whole of the pensions system had been centralised in an enormous old wartime hospital outside Newcastle, it was the centre chosen for the first step for the Welfare State into the world of electronic mechanisation. That too would later lead to problems.

The early computers were batch systems, which meant they held information centrally and divulged it only by printing it out. A query arising in a local office had to be sent physically to North Fylde, where war pensions were handled, or to the other places chosen to house the new technology. There they would be processed, usually overnight, and the result physically shipped back again. And after their own fashion they worked well. In these early days of computerisation, there was no talk – and nor would there be for years to come – of re-organising the system to fit the new technology. The social security computers were not designed to alter the structure of the operation in any way, but simply to relieve the work burden by carrying out some of the more routine tasks previously done by an army of bored clerks. In other words, the computers fitted into the existing system, not the other way round, as would to some extent later be the case.

By the early 1960s, the pressures for more computer power were just as great as they would be later on, even if the logical extension of what had been set in motion was only vaguely understood. For some time the Macmillan government had been under pressure to introduce a new pensions scheme to match the more imaginative proposals of the Crossman plan, largely devised by Professor Richard Titmuss, who was one of the leading intellectual influences on the post-war Welfare State. The Labour Party proposed a generous – and expensive – State scheme, funded by a high rate of contributions from employees, employers and from government. The funds, Labour promised, would be used to invest in private business, which had a certain electoral appeal, although it was dismissed by the Tories as a form of 'back-door nationalisation'. In 1961, the Conservative government produced its more modest reply: a graduated pensions scheme to supplement the basic State retirement pension, with an upper limit of £15 a week as opposed to Labour's £40. The computers at Newcastle, introduced to record the new graduated contributions, proved their worth, and were extended during the 1960s to calculate pensions, a tedious task for clerks.

The new Labour government of 1964 still proposed sweeping changes to the State pension, but there were other priorities and serious financial constraints, both pre- and post-devaluation in October 1967. The Heath government of 1970 also proposed reforms, but it too became sidetracked. For a time it was more interested in the possibilities of combining family support and the tax system as a means of tackling the complex and expensive issue of family poverty. The days of the Macmillan spending spree had also long gone, and the focus now was on those in immediate need of more help. In 1971, a new income-related benefit was introduced to boost the income of families with a working head – family income supplement. It set the pattern for the 1970s, which became, as the civil servants remarked tiredly, 'another year, another benefit'.

National assistance, however, was the real growth area. This was originally introduced in 1948 as a safety net underpinning the new social insurance and other welfare measures. It was never envisaged as the main spearhead of the Welfare State which it, and its successor, supplementary benefit, would later develop into. In 1948, a million claimants and their families depended on national assistance. In 1966, when the Wilson government abolished it, there were two million. The new supplementary benefit, designed to be both more attractive to recipients – in an attempt to reduce the social stigma of being on benefit, the government introduced a legal entitlement to it – and simpler, was soon under the same pressure as its predecessor. The numbers of recipients went on growing: 3 million by 1978 and 4.3 million by 1983.

Because this book is to a large extent an examination of the computerisation of this part in particular of the welfare system, it is worth pausing a moment on supplementary benefit or, as it later became known, income support. In its earlier years, most of the recipients were pensioners, sick or disabled people – essentially those who fell through the cracks in the other benefit schemes. In practice, however, it was discovered that there were many more cracks than the planners thought possible, and over the years the scheme was widened to include assistance with housing costs, help through school meals, and the abatement of prescription and other charges for low-income households. The result, as one of the many Green Papers that appeared in the 1980s remarked, was 'a network of cash and benefits in kind that meet many needs but which, in attempting to cater for so many individual circumstances, are complex to administer and difficult for people to understand.'

By the mid-1970s, the character of those claiming supplementary benefit had changed in a wholly unexpected direction: recipients were now largely unemployed or one-parent families, with rather more volatile circumstances than those of the old-style pensioners, sick or disabled. The government, when it swapped national assistance for supplementary benefit in 1966, actually assumed it would greatly reduce the need for any additional payments. In fact, as unemployment began to rise and become more a feature of contemporary Britain, the opposite was true. By 1974, one in three of the unemployed was getting a weekly addition, and the number of single payments for special needs exceeded three out of ten supplementary benefit cases. For non-pensioners, mainly families, over 60% were now getting additional payments.

There was another significant problem which again was unforeseen: the 1966 scheme, although intended to make benefit a matter of legal entitlement for everyone, also contained a large discretionary element, which had the effect of making it still more difficult to administer. The Supplementary Benefit Commission warned in 1975 that this could lead to a breakdown in reliable administration. 'Pretty soon,' said the Commission's chairman, Professor David Donnison, 'the more hard-pressed officers would be having to make their own simplification in order to cope with the work ... We had perhaps a couple of years in which to achieve some nationwide agreement which would lead to constructive and orderly changes.'

This tended to be the pattern of development in Britain's social security system after the war: a new benefit or a reform designed to upgrade and simplify the old one would lead to unexpected demands and bring in new recipients, straining an already overstretched administrative system still further, until another reform, designed to rectify the situation, made it still worse. Special payments for extra needs, such as fuel and laundry, were introduced for 'exceptional' needs under the old national assistance scheme, but by the end they had become the norm, with six in every ten claiming them. 'Each reform tried to redefine the extent to which the scheme sought to meet the varying needs of its claimants through additional payments on top of basic, weekly rates,' explained a government Green Paper later. But whatever the Department did, still the additional payments grew.

Barbara Castle's new pension scheme, with a strong earnings-related element (thus abandoning a key principle of Beveridge) and with full pensions paid after twenty years, finally came into effect in 1978. Without the machines at Newcastle, it could not have happened. The Newcastle computers had by then long been a feature of the Department, displayed to politicians and other dignitaries as the very latest in technology: people would be taken to gawk as the big ICL machines sent out payable orders to the value of up to £30 million an hour, or £500,000 a minute. Sir Michael Partridge, a senior civil servant and now the Department's Permanent Secretary, remembers as a young civil servant taking around a senior Treasury mandarin who, watching this process in awe, remarked, 'Now I begin to see how this department is actually creating the national debt!'

The relative ease with which pensions were computerised was to lead to major problems on the supplementary benefit front. Because pensions are calculated months in advance, and paid regularly, a centralised computer which will record contributions, calculate benefit due, and then print out the pension books, works perfectly well. But the shorter-term benefits, including unemployment pay, particularly where there is an element of discretion, proved much more difficult to transfer to the new technology – and because of their growing complexity, just as urgent. It required an entirely different treatment. 'If someone suddenly turns up at a social security office and says he has to speak to someone because he's just been made unemployed and he needs some help, it can't be dealt with hundreds of miles away,' explained an official later. 'You've got to have a system which can keep his record and his claim and produce the money very quickly, and it has to go through a very complicated set of rules to do that.'

Putting those rules and regulations onto a computer was a far more difficult task than the routine one of sending out pension books. A trained clerk could actually work out a short-term benefit fairly quickly, once he had all the information he required. The problem was he did not have easy access to all that information. A computer system could provide much of the information needed – and do the calculation as well.

The Department was only too well aware of the growing pressure on resources, and the fact that only a major leap in automation could get it out of a hole that was getting progressively deeper. In the early 1960s, the Department, looking blearily forward to the demands that would hit it over the next decade, set out to develop its own computer system which would relieve the pressure on its increasingly demoralised staff, and at the same time respond to the growing pressures for cost-savings and greater efficiency. Because Newcastle was the source of all computer wisdom in the Department, it was to the wizards of Newcastle that the senior officials in London turned. At this point, no one seems to have nurtured the slightest doubt as to their ability to come up with the answer. Nor did it occur to anyone to think of looking outside the Department for advice or expertise. This would be a homegrown solution to a problem which only the civil servants felt they understood. They had a degree of justification on their side: some of the Department's own people were as good as anyone in the outside world, as they would go on to prove as the Operational Strategy developed. Some of the key figures involved in the strategy were also involved in this early attempt: Phil Dunn, Mike Fogden, Alan Healey and George Bardwell, all of them destined to become major players in the computerisation programmes of the 1980s, began programming for the DHSS at this time. This group did not lack brains or expertise; but it did lack experience of such large on-line systems.

This first attempt at computerising benefit was centred on Reading, more convenient for London than Newcastle, but also another, although more minor, computer centre in the organisation. The assembled team which began work in Reading in the autumn of 1963 had even more confidence in their own problem-solving capacity than their superiors in Alexander Fleming House, the ugly 1960s building which had become the DHSS's headquarters. They had, up to that time, accomplished all the Department had asked of them, and if this project seemed more complex than anything that had gone before, no one felt it was beyond their capacity. 'They had become a bit arrogant up in Newcastle,' says a former official. 'And they weren't very interested in listening to the demands of the people who would have to use the system.'

The Reading experiment, as it became known, started hopefully enough. A new building was commandeered, and the brightest of the computer people were seconded from Newcastle and elsewhere to get it off the ground. The technology had moved on from the big-batch punched-card system used at Newcastle, and the experts opted for the very latest: huge manganese alloy disks, the size of a coffee table, read by a head which ran across them. By the end of three years, the team had devised what Sir Michael Partridge describes as 'the most splendid and elaborate computerised programme of the day'. Technically it was magnificent. But when it was tested in a local office, where it was designed to be used, it didn't work. 'The trouble was the computer was too good,' says Partridge. 'It was so good that if anything went wrong at any stage it spewed out a lot of paper asking people to check it. If you hadn't replied in twenty-four hours, you got another bit of paper, and the office was just getting drowned in paper. It was a beautiful bit of computering, but it was far too complex. So it was scrapped.'

Not without repercussions, however: it was the first failure for the Department's experts, and a serious blow to their morale. It was also a whip with which the Treasury would for evermore beat the DHSS when it came looking for funding for further experiments. 'It was a big disappointment, a big set-back to the Department because it was the first big thing we had tackled on our own,' says a senior civil servant involved with it. Many of the experts, removed from Newcastle to Reading, didn't want to go back, and they didn't have to – they were in the centre of Britain's Silicon Valley, which was beginning to develop, and they had a skill for which there was an almost infinite demand in the private sector. They drifted away, depriving the Department of some of its better computer brains.

For those who stayed there was plenty to do. In 1975, they had to begin writing a new national insurance recording system programme for the introduction of Barbara Castle's new earnings-related pensions, which were administered from Newcastle. Then, separately, they computerised the new child benefit, also administered centrally from Newcastle. None of this tackled the computerisation of benefits (mainly short-term benefits and supplementary benefit and, later, income support) from local offices, but it took several years and in that time there was no capacity for touching the problems the Reading experiment had failed to solve.

But the need to computerise the hundreds of local offices, coping desperately with the flood of new benefits, was still there – and growing all the time. The Department was gradually getting snowed under, with complaints rising, and the reputation of Britain's once much-vaunted social security system sinking. The way in which benefits were organised made it worse – and a monumental task to automate. There was for a start a bewildering array of forms: some 8000 internal non-standard forms and 12,000 external ones. Different benefits were paid at different counters in the local offices, with little overlap or staff expertise. 'Contributory benefit sections were further divided into separate groups dealing with incapacity benefits, pensions, contributions and disablement benefit,' said Helen Magetts in a paper for the Royal Institute of Public Administration. 'This meant that at no point in their dealing with the DHSS were claimants treated as "whole people" but only according to the benefit being claimed.' If a person, wishing to claim a number of different benefits – as many did – walked into a local social security office, they had to make a separate claim for each one. Sometimes they could not be handled in one office, but had to go to another. Behind the counters, the clerks looked at the different claims, assessed them, and dealt with them – without any reference to the other claims the person had made, possibly at the counter next door.

Ministers and officials were increasingly under attack for the quality of service they offered, and with good reason. The social security system, which had set off with such high ideals after the war, was now becoming identified with dingy and depressing offices, a vast and inefficient bureaucracy, delays and long queues, demoralised and rude staff – and for a large number of errors, brought about by the inability to keep up with the paperwork. The typical social security office – and there were over 500 of them – was awash with files, piled up on every desk, with dozens of harried clerks searching for the piece of information they wanted. Careless or demoralised staff often popped a file into the wrong drawer or replaced it in the wrong cabinet. There were fundamental nonsenses at the heart of the system: for instance unemployment pay was (and is) a DSS* benefit, in the sense that that department is responsible for the policy. But it is administered – and paid – by the Department of Employment through another 1000 unemployment benefit offices, using a computer system built and run by the DSS.

The system was also wide open to a new phenomenon of the social security system: fraud. 'People were able to go from one office to another making identical claims without it being picked up,' says an official.

After the failure of the Reading experiment, officials persevered when they could. Geoffrey Otton, later the permanent secretary, recognising the limitations of his own experts, brought in outside consultants to advise. The firm was Hoskyns, then headed by John Hoskyns, who later ran Mrs Thatcher's policy unit in Number 10 Downing Street. Hoskyns, after looking at the problem, advised that the general direction of producing an on-line system, with terminals in the local offices feeding off a centralised system, was the only way to go. It also recognised the formidable problems in the way of achieving it.

Some good would come from the Reading operation: a national unemployment benefit system (known as NUBS 1), run from computers in Reading and Livingston, was based on its technology. Years later, when unemployment soared from half a million to over three million, officials, notably Otton, could claim it as a 'tremendous success story' (which it is – it is still running efficiently, twenty years later). But it was way short of what was wanted for supplementary benefit.

In 1977, ministers agreed to let the Department have another go at developing the integrated system everyone agreed was now desperately needed. Again the place chosen was Reading, and again it was a pilot scheme, with the programming and technical skills drawn largely from Newcastle. Called Computerisation and Mechanisation of Local Office Tasks,

*In July 1988 the Department of Health and Social Security (DHSS) ceased to exist and two ministries – the Department of Health (DOH) and the Department of Social Security (DSS) – were created.

within weeks it was simply referred to under the acronym CAMELOT, and soon no one could remember what it stood for. This was a more ambitious project than the original Reading one, with the civil servants this time determined to learn the lessons of the last failure. 'We said, OK we won't let computer experts handle this,' says Partridge. 'What we'll do is we'll have teams of people in from local offices who will tell us how they do it, and they will help us devise the system. At each stage we'll test it to see if it works.'

At the same time the Department was trying to simplify the benefit system as much as possible. CAMELOT was designed to produce a programme for handling supplementary benefit and other short-term benefits in local offices. But at this stage it was peripheral to something much more fundamental that was taking place in the Department: a complete rethink of where it was going and how it was going to get there. Civil servants who had stumbled bewildered through the growth days of the previous thirty years were determined they would bring some order to the last twenty years of the century. This phase had formally got under way in 1977, at the same time as CAMELOT was in the planning stage.

The central person involved was Norman Clarke, who in September 1976 was made Director of Establishments, which meant he was responsible for personnel, training and industrial relations – a big task given that, even after 20,000 job cuts over the previous decade, the Department still employed over 100,000 people. Clarke, unlike Otton, was a social security expert: although he had spent the previous decade working on the health side of the Department, he had spent years working in the National Assistance Board before that. In the autumn of 1978, Otton rang him. A senior official in Newcastle, George Wilson, had written a paper saying there should be a ten-year look ahead at the pressures under which the Department would have to operate. Otton explained that there had been previous attempts at such projecting, but they had all run into the sands. Now he was proposing something more far-reaching: a working party, which would attempt to determine how the Department could cope with the pressures in an operational sense. Would

Clarke head the working party? The concept, he explained, would be to come up with a strategy for planning Britain's social security operations – not, he emphasised, policy, which was endlessly discussed around the Department, but operations, the actual delivery of benefit to the client. It was to be an operational strategy rather than a policy strategy.

Although the task was unusual, the group Clarke formed was fairly standard Civil Service stuff. It included the policy-makers, the regional directorate, the finance people, representatives from Newcastle, from North Fylde – and of course the computer people. 'I don't want to put any one group in charge of it,' Otton told Clarke, explaining why he wanted him, a relative neutral among the different groups in the Department, to take the chair.

The group was given the title of the Social Security Operational Strategy Working Group, and was soon known less reverently as 'Sausages'. Clarke had no knowledge of computers, but at this point that scarcely mattered. 'We didn't start off with how are we going to computerise the social security system,' says Clarke. 'We started off with what sort of service is it we want to deliver operationally in x years hence.' Later, the mythology in the Department would suggest otherwise, and even the Comptroller and Auditor General's report records that the object of the strategy at this time was to review the needs 'for the administration of social security, particularly in local offices, with a view to using new technology to improve operational efficiency and service to the public'. Clarke, chairing that committee, is clear that was not the case – although it would become so. His group started out by meeting for two solid days each month in one of the many different headquarter buildings owned by the Department. His own office at the time was in Alexander Fleming House. Clarke called it a 'group grope' in the sense that its object was to try to work out 'where we were, what sort of service we were delivering, what was going to happen anyway – because you can always look one or two years ahead in terms of likely policy changes – and where you want to get to. So we definitely didn't set off, as everyone later seemed to think, with a mission to computerise social security.'

Nor, again in contrast to later views, was the strategy designed to save manpower, although that was already becoming a major factor in the Department. It was much more free-ranging and unfocused than that – which made the early discussions somewhat nebulous at times. By the fifth meeting of this group, frustration had begun to set in, as the group seemed to talk endlessly without coming to any conclusions. One of those present recalls a member thumping the table and shouting, 'We're going around in circles', and someone else replying, 'Faced with the task we've been given, I don't know in which other direction we could go.'

Nonetheless, however slowly and painfully, the group was going somewhere: it was feeling its way towards producing what would later be called, grandly but simply, a 'strategy for social security operations', the implications of which would be far more significant than most of those devising it guessed. By 1979, as the computer team in Reading was beginning to work up CAMELOT, the working party had produced what Clarke called a 'template for the future', or more formally, 'a list of desiderata', all of which seemed fairly obvious, all aimed simply at providing the public with a better, more accessible, more accurate and more efficient service. Yet it served a useful and important function, basically by proving to the senior officials (and their ministers) that the Department was not doing what it was supposed to, and furthermore that it was not even headed remotely in the direction in which it wanted to go.

Clarke reported to a steering committee above him, headed by Alec Atkinson, the permanent secretary in charge of social security at the time, that, although the desiderata looked terribly obvious, they had a purpose. 'We're in the business of influencing the minds, or the pulse, of people,' he said. 'I agree it is all terribly self-evident. Now you just sit back and analyse everything that has happened in the past fifteen years, and ask has it pointed in the direction we want to go? Not to a precise degree, but even vaguely in that direction? And the answer is NO! And therefore you've got to change your way of thinking. If these desiderata are so obvious, why are we not there now?

We really have to start thinking about how we're going to do it.'

Clarke had, albeit slowly, felt his way to what he announced as 'the only answer – information technology. You have to computerise.'

The first couple of years of Clarke's group had run parallel with CAMELOT, but curiously their paths barely touched. Clarke knew little about CAMELOT, was not involved in its progress or its problems, yet inevitably the direction his group was pursuing led in the direction of automating the whole system.

Within a year, therefore, Clarke's group had groped its way to the conclusions that others, including Otton, had already reached: there was no question of the Department coping with the increasing complexity of demands on its services without computerisation. They also formalised another concept which had been growing in the Department for years, but which no one had properly given voice to: that of the 'whole person', which meant simply that all the information required on a person claiming benefit – any benefit – would be available on a single electronic file. It was nonsense to have half a dozen different files in different places on the same person.

In retrospect these simple conclusions seem blindingly obvious, but in a department which was doing well just to keep its head above water, there was not much time – or much encouragement – for conceptual thinking. The 'whole person' concept and computerisation were of course inextricably linked, and from this time on would be the central driving force in the reform of the efficiency of Britain's Welfare State. 'The ideal,' said a Department working paper in 1980, explaining the 'whole person' concept to a sceptical and impatient public, 'would be that one claim would lead to the combined payment of all the benefits to which that person was entitled; that advice about all benefits would be available at a single point; and that information about changes of circumstances reported to one specific point would be applied without further action by the beneficiary to all processing points.'

It was one thing reaching such profound conclusions and rather another implementing them. Experiments in the

Department had already shown how difficult it was to handle different benefits on one claim form, particularly where multi-purpose means tests were involved – as, by the late 1970s, they often were. Around 60% of those in receipt of supplementary benefits were also claiming national insurance benefits, and over 40% of those below pension age were receiving child benefit. Nevertheless, from the late 1970s on the Department accepted that the 'whole person' approach must be the direction in which it would go – and the only way to achieve anything approximating to it was through sophisticated computer data bases and an even more sophisticated modern communications system.

In tackling this large problem of how to get where the Department now knew it wanted to go, much hinged on the success or failure of CAMELOT – and the omens there were not good. By 1980, the work performed by some of the DHSS computers was impressive enough, with the Department's in-house experts fully capable of designing and installing the relatively straightforward system. The Unemployed Benefit System, which had grown out of the much-maligned Reading experiment, was now expanding without great strain to handle six times the numbers it had originally been designed for. There were separate computer systems for different benefits, most of them working efficiently enough, but as the Operational Strategy review would later note, in an acid aside, they were 'heterogeneous and relatively uncoordinated'. Personal information on individuals was held, on average, in five different places, none of them accessible to the other. There were some on-line links to the pensions computers in Newcastle, but overall the system was a higgledy-piggledy collection of incompatible systems which had grown without much plan or co-ordination, and which offered little hope of getting the Department out of its growing mess.

There was now another driving factor behind reform: in 1979 the Labour government had gone and the Thatcher era had begun. The new Secretary of State for Health and Social Services was Patrick Jenkin, who had worked in industry and was bringing a much more hard-headed approach to the

Department's work. Cuts in government spending had actually begun under Jim Callaghan, Denis Healey and Tony Crosland in 1976, but the general feeling persisted that under Labour these would be restored once the economy improved again. From June 1979 onwards, no one believed that: Mrs Thatcher and her ministers had come to power promising sweeping changes of the whole government machine, which everyone understood to mean more value for less money. The Conservatives' 1979 manifesto had actually been remarkably short on specific commitments as far as the Welfare State was concerned, simply including generalised pledges to make better use of available resources, cut back the bureaucracy, and maintain spending on the National Health Service (which it did). There had however been plenty of discussions before the election, notably along the lines of increasing private provision of services and the wider use of charges throughout the social services, mostly reflecting the work of the free-market think-tank, the Institute of Economic Affairs.

If there were any lingering doubts that Thatcher would flinch once she was in 10 Downing Street, they abruptly vanished with Sir Geoffrey Howe's first Budget. 'The underlying assumption of continuous expansion which had lasted for 30 years since the Second World War had come to an end' in the field of social welfare, wrote Timothy Raison in his book *Tories and the Welfare State.* With Labour, he added, the assumption was that the cuts were being made very reluctantly. 'Under Mrs Thatcher the argument was that people were entitled to keep more of their own earnings.'

Cuts, of course, were intended, and indeed real cuts, at least in expectations, were made. Child benefit was frozen from April 1979 to November 1980, saving some £250 million. The earnings-related supplement was abandoned, and the rise in unemployment and sickness benefit fixed at five percentage points less than the increase in inflation. There were other changes too, all of them justified by the government on the grounds that any attempt to control the overall level of public spending must include the social security budget, simply because it was so large.

The total saving was officially estimated at around £2 billion a year by 1982–3, equivalent to 2p off the basic rate of income tax. But these were cuts only off the planned total – the actual amount spent on the Welfare State continued to rise even under Thatcher. Demography and rising unemployment saw to that: the number of retirement pensioners rose from 8.53 million to 9.07 million between 1979 and 1983; the numbers receiving unemployment benefit doubled from 570,000 to 1.2 million in the first two years of the new Tory government and would go on rising above 3 million; and the numbers receiving short-term supplementary allowances, designed to top up the basic supplementary benefit, expanded from 925,000 to 1.8 million. In line with these, the numbers receiving rate rebates and other benefits went up more or less proportionately.

All of this would create still greater pressure for savings in the Department, and provide Norman Clarke and his cogitating committee with a reason for moving faster.

Patrick Jenkin lost little time in translating the Clarke thoughts into a working paper called 'A Strategy for Social Security Operations' that year, writing a foreword to it himself. It pointed to the strain that the social security operations were now under, how it would get worse, and then added that advances in computer and telecommunications technology were creating new opportunities for advance during the 1980s.

This paper is in many ways the seminal work on what developed into the whole of the Operational Strategy, under which, over the next twenty years, the system whereby contributions were collected, advice provided, claims for benefit taken, amounts calculated and payments made would be determined. When it appeared in November 1980, Jenkin apologised for its thinking being at 'a very early stage', but reckoned it was worth making the debate public. 'It seems sensible as well as right that there should be an early opportunity for anyone who wishes to comment, or who has a contribution to make, to do so.' The paper stressed the importance of 'technological progress', which lay at the heart of the strategy, but he was cautious about raising expectations: 'We can only benefit from technology that we can afford, and there will be other claims on the resources available in five and ten years' time, as now.'

The paper set out the scale of the task the Department faced: ten new cash benefits had been introduced in the 1970s, bringing the total to thirty-four; there were new pension schemes, and the complete recasting of the earnings-related contributory system, with increasing use of means-testing. The highly complex means-tested supplementary benefit scheme now required 37,000 people to administer it at a cost of £280 million, almost three times the cost of delivering pensions to 9 million people.

The paper now laid out the bones of the computerisation of the system that would later provide the framework from which Andersen Consulting would work: all computers would be concentrated at a few large centres, with direct links to local offices. Every local office would have on-line access to a central record, or national index. But how it would be achieved, Jenkin and his officials – mainly Otton, Partridge and Clarke – had little clear idea. Although the alarm bells were already sounding over CAMELOT, the paper reflected the hopes of the officials that all would be well with it: its response time was 2–3 seconds on individual terminals, said the paper proudly, as it elaborated on the technological leaps between this magnetic disk technology and the old magnetic tape batch-system computers. 'The advantages it can offer in meeting the needs of the Department are potentially very great indeed.' Later on it added that this pilot project 'should go live in 1981, with a view to possible national implementation during the mid-1980s.' It was a forlorn hope.

If officials were able to convince Jenkin that CAMELOT would work, behind the scenes they were only too aware that there were problems. In the beginning, the project, like the Reading experiment before it, worked well, certainly well enough to persuade ministers and the Department to continue throwing funds at it. It did suffer one major problem, however: the technological revolution was now in full swing in Britain and anyone with a computer background commanded a premium, particularly in the Reading area. All the time it was in progress, some of its best staff were being poached, and turnover was high. But there was a more fundamental problem too: those that remained were expert in the type of systems operated in Newcastle, which were already a generation behind the latest technology. In the latter half of the 1970s, information technology had taken not one but several quantum leaps, and in effect the thinking being applied was 1960s rather than 1970s thinking. It was one thing to design a computer system, but very much another to make it work in the circumstances in which it would be used. No one involved had ever managed a project, and no one fully understood the in-built flaws that were part of CAMELOT from the start. At the Department, the senior civil servants happily assumed all was well as the parts of project that were tested seemed to work when they were tried out in local offices. After all, they argued, this was a user-led system, designed by the customer, as opposed to an engineering-led system designed by the programmers.

It was in 1981, when they got to what is called the 'suite' testing stage, where individual parts were required to work together, that CAMELOT fell apart. The programmes that had worked in test conditions simply did not gel together. At first, the senior DHSS managers believed that these were typical start-up problems which could be solved with a modest amount of effort and time. Gradually, however, the doubts grew. 'I was in charge of local offices and I started to feel that all was not right,' says Partridge. 'It wasn't just teething problems, as people said. It was slipping month after month and there was something fundamentally wrong.'

The experts from Newcastle were slow to accept it. Nor, as the Public Accounts Committee would later conclude, were they being properly managed by the Department, which had even less expertise in this area. As 1981 wore on, officials began to think the unthinkable – the Department would not get it right using its own resources. They would have to look outside.

It was to be some months before the full message began to sink in. In retrospect, the DHSS managers would kick themselves for their own naivety, but at the time they had few yardsticks. First of all, they had, despite the failure of the

Reading experiment, been convinced that they could produce the system from within. Even at this stage, they were not as concerned as they should have been: their own people might have failed, but they believed the building blocks were in place and, with a bit of extra expertise, the whole thing could be made to work.

The consultants, brought in by Partridge, soon disillusioned everyone. The work done, they announced, was fundamentally flawed. If the Reading experiment had produced a computer that was too sophisticated for the work it was expected to do, CAMELOT, designed in effect by the user, suffered from the other extreme: the local offices had asked too much of the computers and had made their work too complex to computerise. The task set was beyond the programming skills of the team, and probably of anyone. The equipment they were working with, and the programmes they had designed, were never going to be able to cope with the workload which had increased even while they were designing it.

Eric Caines, who had by then become the director of regional operations, became one of CAMELOT's principal critics, a factor that did not endear him to his colleagues. 'It was just totally out of control,' he said later. 'There was no match between the real needs of servicing sickness benefit and invalidity benefit claims. The whole system had become grossly inflated, costs were just running away, we were collecting too much information, the technical infrastructure was proving too much of a nightmare and there was really no tight project control.' It was, he adds with some sympathy for the people running it, 'very difficult for a team sitting in the middle to say to the head of a policy division "I'm sorry, we're not going to do that." And so all sorts of things were added on, and the complexity and scale and costs were growing out of all recognition. And so we just scuppered it and tried to learn some lessons from it.'

Partridge now had the task of going to Sir Geoffrey Otton, a keen supporter of CAMELOT, to deliver the bad news. 'The consultants say it won't work,' he told him. 'I think we should call a halt to it. We're going to have a lot of egg on our faces and we're going to have to go along and say we've failed for the second time in ten years.'

For Otton it was a particularly severe blow. Otton, a tall, gentle man with receding hair and a donnish appearance, had joined the Home Office after Cambridge in 1950 and had worked his way up the ranks from assistant principal to assistant under-secretary of state running the government's child care programme. Then abruptly, in 1971, child care was transferred to the DHSS and Otton went with it. His career, far from withering as he half expected in the new environs, took off. His fellow civil servants were steeped in the lore and (for Otton) the mystique of family support, pension contributions and earnings-related benefits – all baffling to a Home Office man. Otton found what he thought was his own niche – but which soon turned into the central stream of the whole department. He became fascinated with improving efficiency through information technology, and it was he who had tried to take the lessons from the Reading experiment into CAMELOT. He was not alone, of course, but as he rose up the ranks Otton became one of the leading advocates for greater automation in the whole Civil Service. Now he had to contend with the collapse of CAMELOT.

In December 1981, the DHSS formally reported that CAMELOT 'as currently conceived' could not result in a useful or operable system. The consultants had made a number of recommendations, too late to save CAMELOT, but with some lessons for the future: the Department was going to need proper technical support. It was also going to have to develop a number of projects separately but as part of an overall plan. 'We decided then to step back and look at the whole thing,' says Partridge. What came from this was the absolute realisation that the Department could not do it on its own. It simply did not have the expertise, or the people. Time and money had both been wasted trying to develop systems to computerise local offices which were out of date and inadequate before the work had even begun.

CHAPTER TWO

ENTER ANDERSEN

The early years of the Thatcher government had seen some changes to the social security system, but for the moment the Tories were concentrating their attentions elsewhere. The administration's attitude generally to the Welfare State was governed principally by its desire to hold down public expenditure, rather than by any strong desire for wholesale reform. The recession, of course, had forced the social security budget up, but even so it was still £2 billion below what it would have been without cuts. Much of the focus in these years was on the National Health Service, which ranked only behind the economy as a matter of public concern. Each winter, the NHS produced yet another crisis, forcing the government to put in more money, and making it a far more pressing issue than the social security system. In December 1981, Margaret Thatcher made her famous commitment to preserving the NHS when she told the Commons 'the principle that adequate health care should be provided for all regardless of ability to pay must be the function of any arrangements for financing the NHS'. She would later repeat that at the Tory Party conference in Brighton the following year, prefaced by the phrase 'The National Health Service is safe with us' (not 'safe in our hands', as she was often misquoted as saying).

But if expenditure on health and social security could not be cut, that did not mean it should be left entirely alone. The emphasis right across the government spectrum in these years was to develop private facilities, encourage the provision of hospital pay-beds, assisted places in schools and private insurance schemes. The principles of private provision of services, or even contracting out of public-sector work, were not easy to apply to the social security system, but the Tories were determined to try. Work done by the Institute of Economic Affairs had long advocated the extension of the use of charges throughout the social services. Nothing very much happened before 1981, but after that the continuing financial pressures gave a new momentum to cost savings and to privatisation.

The Chancellor, Sir Geoffrey Howe, set this out in a speech in July 1982:

'There are powerful reasons why we must be ready to consider how far private provision and individual choice can supplement, or in some cases possibly replace, the role of government in health, social security and education. Most of these reasons are economic.'

The 'economic' reasons he gave were, of course, ones of public expenditure or, as he put it, 'the need to reform our system of social provision would be pressing on public spending grounds alone.' The thrust of his speech was directed at health and the local authorities, but Sir Geoffrey left no doubt that the government would apply the philosophy to social security as well, if only it could find a way. 'We must meet the increasingly frustrated demands of society in a fair and efficient way.'

This was the mood in which the officials at the DHSS set out to put their Operational Strategy, still no more than an imaginative concept, into effect. Civil servants such as Otton and Clarke, both exceptionally bright and clever men, were at their best in conceptualising. Clarke's 'group grope' had actually contained some deep and fundamental thinking, and had forced the Department, and the rest of government, to face up to the reality that the service they were giving to the public had actually been deteriorating for more than twenty years, and in all likelihood would go on deteriorating for the next twenty. For years it had been hidden to some extent as governments threw more money at it, hiring more and more people to deliver an absurd panoply of benefits in conditions which no private operation could survive in. The senior officials also knew that the answer – the only answer – on the operational side was computerisation on a scale never seen before in Europe, let alone in Britain. It was when it came to putting that conclusion into practice that all their experience and training failed them. Otton had tried with CAMELOT, and its failure was now such a public one, raised often in the House of Commons, examined by the Public Accounts Committee and by the office of the Comptroller and Auditor General, that it was a huge discouragement to try again. For his part, Clarke took the view that his role had been to decide on the strategy, but he had no knowledge nor any interest in computers and preferred to leave the implementation to someone else. In the 1980 working paper he had laid out the bones of a new computer system, but he had no clear idea how to take it beyond that. Meanwhile, the service was still getting worse, to the point where politically the quality of the social security system was hurting, bad service being inextricably associated in the public mind with lack of resources.

In 1981, Patrick Jenkin had moved to the Department of Industry to be replaced by Norman Fowler, who was to guide the project through the mid-1980s. There were changes in the Civil Service too. Clarke had been promoted and was now the principal establishment officer with full responsibility for the whole of social security operations, and for the establishments of both social security and health within the DHSS. Within that much wider brief, the Operational Strategy still featured prominently on his agenda, as recognised by the fact that later, when a new Operational Strategy Steering Committee was created, Otton made him chairman of it.

The steering committee was in effect an extension of Clarke's original 'Sausages' group, which would soon be condemned by some of the more abrasive characters on it, such as the director of regional organisation, Eric Caines. Of all the people, consultants or civil servants, involved in the Operational Strategy, Caines was to be one of the most central and important. He was – and is – a most unusual civil servant, both in appearance and attitude. He flouted the conventional Civil Service style of dress and appearance. Long hair framed a florid face dominated by a large bristling moustache; his shirts and ties often made Clarke and Otton wince. Where Otton went to Cambridge and Partridge to Oxford, Caines went to Leeds. His early career in the Civil Service had been meteoric, but by his middle years he had acquired a reputation as a man who was highly effective but was not a team player – a loose cannon in a society that liked an orderly ship. He had been with the National Coal Board for a number of years, which, although it was a nationalised industry, still gave him the kind of hard-nosed managerial experience that was rare in the Civil Service. In many ways he was the ideal man to take on the job of translating Clarke's blueprint into reality, but there was tension between him and other senior officials, and Clarke often found him too abrasive.

Where Caines attacked Clarke's steering committee as too academic and removed from reality, Clarke defended it. 'I saw it as a way of keeping people informed, and enabling them to discuss problems and have confidence in what was going on. Nobody could claim they were taken by surprise,' he says.

That was certainly true: everyone now knew the problems. But in the early 1980s there was remarkably little attention paid to solving them. Since the Jenkin working paper of 1980, the Department had received hundreds of submissions, papers and other thoughts on how to take the strategy on, and in the summer of 1982, two years after they had written the first working paper, Otton and Clarke started work on a fuller and more formal Green Paper. In the past year, Lynda Chalker, the parliamentary under-secretary responsible for social security, had held a two-day seminar to seek the advice of experts from industry, the computer world and the universities; there had been a continual round of meetings with suppliers of computer equipment and communications systems and much else. Now Clarke pulled it all together in a Green Paper which would flesh out the earlier one. Clarke's Strategy Study Team had even employed its own consultants, Software Sciences, to look at the design of the system. The computer firm Logica had also carried out a study which had recommended that, instead of going to a fully integrated system, the best course would be to automate 'in situ', using micro-computers.

The words 'Operational Strategy' had been coined, almost casually, under a previous government and been given currency by a previous Secretary of State. That summer there was some debate as to whether they should stick with it. This would be Norman Fowler's Green Paper, and at one point the civil servants spent some time trying to find a way of giving it a 'Fowler flavour'. In the event, however, the Green Paper was simply called 'Social Security Operational Strategy – A framework for the future'. Although it was still only a consultative paper, it was a much more definitive document than the first one. It is hard now to find, between its austere lines, signs of the underlying battles fought within the Department before it was finally agreed. But they were there nonetheless.

One of these was over the position of Newcastle, which was still very much the heart of the operational side of the whole Department. The Newcastle social security operation was almost a separate department by itself, a huge, sprawling office complex on the edge of the town. In London it was known as the 'barony', but in truth it was more akin to a feudal kingdom, paying dues and lip-service to the court in London, but going about its business in its own way and in its own time. As Britain's shipyards closed and Tyneside became an industrial wasteland in the early 1980s, the DHSS, already the largest employer in the area, became ever more important. But there was another reason for its self-confidence and reluctance to accept direction from London: if computers were to be the answer to the future, then Newcastle had to be at the centre of that answer because by far the majority of the Department's computer systems were based there. It also meant that an industrial relations problem in Newcastle – and they were never far away – could paralyse the whole country.

Otton, who had by now taken over as second permanent secretary in the Department, in charge of social security, was determined that somehow he had to break the power of Newcastle, wean the new systems away from its clutches, and ensure that industrial unrest there could not threaten the system.

This was more than a vague fear. Fresh from the 'winter of discontent' in 1978–9, the Thatcher government had set about breaking the power of the trade unions, not least the public-sector unions. In the first two years of the new government, there were bloody and fruitless battles with the Civil Service unions which came to a head in a lengthy and bitter pay dispute in 1981. Nine separate unions formed a united front and took selective action which focused on the national computer centre in Newcastle. The strikes were eventually called off after the government stepped up its pay offer and established an independent inquiry under a retired judge, Sir John Megaw. Megaw's report appeared in the summer of 1982, and suggested a system of job evaluation, with greater accountability and responsibility. The unions, particularly in Newcastle, hated it, seeing it as encouraging the prevailing winds of market forces. They emerged from this period weaker overall, but in Newcastle the mood grew more militant, and Otton was under orders from his ministers to sideline Newcastle. It must play the least possible part in the Operational Strategy. Much to the disgust of the Newcastle hierarchy, that was implicit in the Green Paper.

There was another factor steering the direction the Green Paper was taking. 1982 was the government's Information Technology Year, and computerisation had become the flavour everywhere. The Inland Revenue was already embarked on a computerisation programme almost as ambitious – but simpler – than that of the DHSS, and ministers increasingly saw it as the one method available for delivering cost cuts.

When the Fowler paper finally appeared in September 1982, the wording again was cautious, with Fowler explaining in his foreword that 'implementation will not be easy, nor will it be cheap. Consequently, it must be tackled with great care, step by step, with regular pauses for evaluation.'

For all its tentative status, the Fowler Green Paper was a thoughtful, well-argued document, setting out the parts of the welfare system which were to be computerised. Principal among these were supplementary benefit, unemployment benefit, and child benefit (which was to fall by the wayside as things got tough later). The central theme of the Green Paper was that the video terminal in the local office had to be at the centre of the system. 'Information would be "input" to the computer through terminals and the "output" would be received in the same way or printed out and sent through the post.' It proposed a central index, covering every person in the country with a National Insurance Number, which would be based near Newcastle. But the Department was not going to place all its eggs in the Newcastle basket. The main operating part of the system would be a series of computer centres placed strategically around the country, which would provide the link for thousands of terminals in the local offices with the support they badly needed. They would hold records, process claims, and even make payments. This would be called the Local Office Project, or LOP, and was the scheme that would occupy a great deal of the time and energy of the Andersen Consulting team. The paper even included a chart setting out the timetable: the first area centre to start up in 1986, the last one in 1990, with national coverage of all the local offices to be achieved by 1991. National coverage of all short-term benefit applications, including unemployment benefit, would not be achieved until 1994 – some dozen years away. By the time everything was on-line and linked together under the strategy, it would be into the next century.

Clarke and his team had costed the schemes in rough outline, and had begun the task of arguing their figures through a reluctant and sceptical Treasury. Fowler was now committing his department to a twenty-year programme that was projected to cost the hefty sum of £700 million, over and above what the Department was already spending on its existing computerisation programme (in the event, the cost would be £1.8 billion by the year 2000, but that was largely because, as the civil servants realised the potential, they added further projects and expanded the system). That, he argued, was actually less than 3% of total administration costs, and a minuscule 0.14% of the vast quantities of benefits the Department paid out.

Against this, there were major savings to be made: £1.9 billion gross or £1.2 billion net. By year eight, the paper projected optimistically, annual savings would exceed costs. How was that to be achieved?

Basically by eliminating the need for some 20,000–25,000 out of the Department's total staff of 100,000. That would begin, if all went according to the schedule – which of course it did not – by 1984, and go on building, with a sharp increase from 1990. These estimates were to prove another of the major miscalculations of the DHSS's Operational Strategy.

In the meantime, there would be some modest improvements in technology in the local offices. They could not get inter-linked terminals for some years, but they could be given micro-computers, as recommended by Logica, which would help marginally, mostly by lifting morale.

There had been another change too, small by comparison with the others, yet nonetheless one for which the thousands of people working in the local offices were suitably grateful. Shopping in Sainsbury's one day, Geoffrey Otton noticed the new bar-coding system the stores group employed on the check-out. By sliding a gun over the code, imprinted on every item sold, the price and identity of the item were automatically registered. Otton became intrigued by it, and soon had a couple of experts studying it. If it worked for frozen peas, why should it not work too for social security files? Why not bar-code each file, and then every time it was moved, the recipient would simply run his reader over it, thus letting a central registry in the office know exactly where it was.

It was a novel, simple and inexpensive idea – and would prove highly successful. The local offices still had as much paperwork as ever, but at least they knew where to find it. Hours of fruitless searching would be eliminated.

By the end of 1982, the outline of the Operational Strategy had been hammered out, published and absorbed. It was time to get on to the serious design and development work, and then to implementing what would be the biggest computerisation programme in Europe, and possibly the world, providing information to the staff of 500 DHSS offices and 800 unemployment benefit offices around the country. To achieve it would require outside help of a kind Department officials only dimly knew existed.

By coincidence, the DHSS had gone outside for consultancy help on a tiny project that August, and in doing so had contacted Andersen Consulting. It was such a minor job that normally Andersen might not have bothered, but at the time the advanced information technology group, headed by Keith Burgess, was running low on work, and saw this as a possible foot-hold on bigger things. 'It was a little study on human interaction with the computer, and we knew the answer,' says an Andersen man. 'We did a pitch, but they didn't want to know the answer – they wanted some psychologist to worry about the problem. You know, sometimes people find the problem much more interesting than the answer.'

But the group had pressed hard for the business, and made an impression, and several of the senior civil servants were keen to get them involved in helping them with their technology. Andersen, of course, knew nothing of this, but began building up its momentum for the bigger contracts that were now expected to flow from the publication of the Green Paper.

In many ways, the Andersen people could scarcely be more different to the civil servants they would soon work alongside. Highly trained, better paid than their Civil Service counterparts, and with much more varied experience, they were also steeped in their craft of solving the problems of the hundreds of companies rushing to modernise themselves in the 1970s and 1980s. Part of the Arthur Andersen & Co. worldwide accounting firm, Andersen Consulting had, since the 1940s, grown from a single office in Chicago to an operation working out of 157 offices in forty-five countries. It was the largest management consultancy in the world but, of even greater interest to the DHSS, it was the leader in the fast-growing information technology field. Through the boom of the 1960s and 1970s, its business had grown at 15% a year, and even through the 1980s would accelerate to a 30% growth rate. In 1982 it employed nearly 6000 professional consultants, advising everyone from Lockheed (on winning a development contract for the Advanced Tactical Fighter) to Boeing (on designing computing systems for shop-floor control) on getting the most sophisticated information systems in the world to function properly, and much else. It worked with leading companies in Japan, Sweden, Germany and, of course, the United States, where its principal base remained. In Britain its growth had been particularly spectacular: 40% a year through most of the 1970s, a rate that would continue, and even accelerate, through the 1980s.

Later the civil servants would remark, in wonderment rather than slightingly, on how easy it was to distinguish an Andersen man from a civil servant. The Civil Service is by no means a lumpen mass, and its staff are as varied in background and education as any other large organisation. Assistant principals, the grade the Andersen people mostly came into contact with, were all graduates. Yet the cultures and attitudes were often a world apart, each side slightly bemused by the other, at least in the early days, before they began to see each other as individuals. 'They were all very high calibre people – that was obvious from the beginning,' says a former civil servant of the Andersen recruits. 'All graduates, and with very good training. But in some ways they were a little inflexible, stamped out of the Andersen cloning machine. They all talked the same – and even looked the same.'

That to an extent was understandable, given the similarity of the backgrounds of the Andersen people, plus the rigorous training they were put through. As one senior man explains: 'We pick from the absolute cream of the university graduates, and we put them through intensive training. In the late 1960s we decided that technology was going to be the key, and that we were going to be the best at it. So we ploughed a huge amount of our investment into technology and technology training. We have the Andersen Consulting university at St Charles, near Chicago, and everyone goes there for an initial three-week intensive training course (and then once or twice a year for the first three or four years of their career). We have a very strong training programme, and technology is embedded into training for all new recruits. Most of the work we got involved in over that period was technology, and we honed and developed our skills on those assignments, and literally became the premier technical consulting organisation in the 1980s. So there is a very regimented approach to training and to self-discipline and work which seems to produce these clones. But they're very, very bright clones.'

'Every client we've ever had where we've put large numbers of young people on the project thinks they've invented the term android,' says another Andersen man. 'We don't mind – it's a good trait of ours.'

What some of the senior officials came to understand was that by buying a firm of consultants you were not just buying the men who came to do the work; you were buying the whole accumulated experience of the firm worldwide, something the computer experts in Newcastle, however clever, could never match.

Nevertheless, the job did not automatically – or even exclusively – go to Andersen. They still had to get it the hard way. On 15 October 1982, a letter, typed on drab DHSS paper and looking for all the world like a letter about unpaid national insurance contributions, arrived at the London offices of Andersen Consulting in Arundel Street, running from the Strand almost down to the Temple. It was headed: 'Social Security Operational Strategy: Management Consultancy'.

The Department, it explained, was seeking a 'Progress Management Consultancy' to help it manage the task of implementing the proposals set out in the Green Paper. It invited Andersen to submit a short written proposal by 5 November. A detailed 'statement of credentials' must be sent by Andersen to the Department immediately. The Department also set out the timetable, which was positively breakneck by government standards: the short-list would be interviewed on 16/17 November, just a month away, and the contract placed five days before Christmas. A sense of urgency was beginning to pervade the Department.

The letter found its way to the desk of the man who would be responsible for putting together the Andersen team which would work on the Department's Operational Strategy, and whose standing in the firm would come to depend on its success or failure.

Keith Burgess at the time was thirty-six, a young partner heading the technology division, and working his way rapidly towards even higher things. Born in September 1946 in Merthyr Tydfil, he was the son of a local hotelier. From the local grammar school (which Neil Kinnock had attended several years before), Burgess went to Bristol University, where he took a degree in physics and then a PhD in solid-state physics – which included the rudiments of electronics.

Burgess joined Andersen in 1971 to undergo the usual intensive training period, including the statutory period in Chicago, but was soon back in London advising the National Health Service on building new hospitals. He spent much of the 1970s around Whitehall, working with various departments, putting early budgetary controls into the Department of Trade and Industry, and with the Treasury, installing systems to monitor public expenditure after the International Monetary Fund was called in in 1976. His Treasury experience, on one of the biggest Andersen jobs around at the time, was to prove invaluable. Afterwards he was sent to British Gas to carry out a major project there. Burgess was coming to the end of a project for the building group Wates, and was anxiously wondering how he would keep his group occupied, when the approach from the DHSS came in. 'I was in the market for a nice, new, interesting client or project,' he said later. For that reason, but also because he had been around Whitehall long enough to guess that this could develop into something larger, he gave the DHSS proposal his full attention. In many ways it seemed perfect for Andersen, with its stress on automated systems, and Burgess, with his Whitehall experience, was ideally suited to lead it. Beside him was a man who would be almost as important as Burgess in the project: Mark Otway, thirty-four years old, was another relatively junior partner, a man skilled in computer systems and technology. Otway had joined Andersen in 1970 after graduating in natural sciences and chemical engineering from Churchill College, Cambridge, and had developed a taste for designing complex technical systems. He had also spent years developing large on-line data-base systems for the distribution industry, and was equally suited to the DHSS task. He was also an excellent foil for the less technologically minded Burgess, who left the architecture of the system to him.

'One of the braver things that Keith did was that he committed two partners for three years,' says an Andersen man, 'on the hope and a prayer that we could turn it into a substantial amount of work. Because if you're a partnership of 16 partners, which we were, and you take an eighth of your partnership away for a client who is only supporting another four people, then that's not very good economics. As it happened it wasn't a problem, but that was the bet that Keith made. And that was a special piece of thinking.'

It was by no means a walkover, however. Initially, the Department approached some fourteen consulting firms, asking them to submit proposals. By November there was a short-list of five, and Burgess now set his heart on winning it. There is a slightly arrogant view inside Andersen Consulting that when it really sets out to get a job, it will get it, and Burgess wanted this one. He devoted the second half of November and early December to preparing his pitch, reading everything he could get his hands on, including the Green Papers, talking to everyone with any knowledge of the Operational Strategy, and preparing examples of work Andersen had done in the past. 'We hit it very hard because there was some tremendous potential to be gained from it, and we had developed a plan to work with their operation (at that stage known, within the Department, as MSC6), and, bang! – we won it just before Christmas and by 17 January 1983 we had started.'

Andersen, however, did not get the whole of the Operational Strategy at that stage. The three-year contract it had been awarded was only part of the work put out to consultants. There was another half to it, which Burgess went after too, but which he lost – as he knew he was destined to. CAMELOT had not been allowed to die as easily as many hoped it would. The team had basically been split in two, one to work on a new unemployment benefit system, the other to continue its work into computerising the DHSS local offices – this time with outside consultants looking over its shoulder. 'You've got a pile of people sitting down there in an office in Reading, and you've sort of killed CAMELOT, so now what do you do with them all?' said one official later. 'This is a big problem. So you see if you can get it right second time round. So they got a new project manager, and they started playing again.'

In its early days the Local Office Project (LOP) was known as 'Son of CAMELOT'. The wags in the Department, later urged on by the Andersen people, who resented this end of the operation, modified that to 'Camelop', particularly when it was hitting problems (as it often was).

At this stage, typical of the history of the automation of Britain's social security system, there were separate operations and separate reporting points. There was the MSC6 group under John Ray, responsible for working on the overall Operational Strategy. But there was also LOP, which in many ways was the centre of any automation programme, run separately from Reading. Both elements wanted consultants, but they did not want the same ones. The Reading project, now headed by Ian Marshall, preferred the American firm Computer Sciences Corporation (CSC), already well advanced on a huge programme to computerise the Inland Revenue.

At the time, Burgess and his team at Andersen knew little of this. 'We tried to bid for both jobs, which in practice would have been easier, because I think we would have had the attention of the people in both places,' said Burgess later. Concentrating on the overall strategy job, Burgess was not able to bring the same focused energy on getting the LOP job, but it wouldn't have mattered anyway – he was never going to get it, at least not at that stage. He did, however, try. 'I only had a three-week window and I had to decide which people I could promise where, and I couldn't play the same people on both projects at the same time. So all told that was going to require dishing out fifteen to twenty people, all of whom would stand there and be interviewed, which because of the size of the practice at the time, we couldn't do. There simply weren't enough people in that kind of time scale for us to be able to deal with it, so we decided the high-ground one was the one to go for. So they gave Reading/LOP to CSC, and I think that that set the whole programme twelve to eighteen months back. If we had been in LOP as well, I think we could have cut out a lot of argument, we could have been one seller of advice, and the work would have moved forward a lot faster. And we would have saved millions – that's the price of open competitive tendering!'

Once again, even though the DHSS had arrived at the right strategy, its implementation of it was far from perfect. It would be several years before strategy and implementation came together, and by then the Department's Operational Strategy would be in some trouble.

CHAPTER THREE

'SPEND MORE TIME *in the* PUB'

As the Andersen team started work for the DHSS, they had little idea how major this project was to become for the partnership. An initial contract for five people for three years gave few clues to the immense task on which they were now embarking. Nor did the terms of reference of their appointment. Basically, Andersen had agreed to advise and assist the DHSS in 'overseeing implementation' of its Social Security Operational Strategy. In particular, it would provide an independent management and technical view of progress, advise the Department on equipment and systems, pinpoint technical problems 'at an early stage' and advise on their solution, and assist in 'establishing design standards for strategy development'. It was all fairly general and run-of-the-mill, standard terms of reference which could have applied to a dozen contracts Andersen was involved in at that time.

What singled it out, however, was the sheer scale of the project. The Department had included a brief introduction to the task, a useful overview of the situation it faced: 24 million beneficiaries of benefit at any one time, 1.2 billion payments a year, 117,000 staff (including the local office staff), and annual administration costs of £1.4 billion. 'Staff rely on over 100 bulky instruction manuals – closely printed, frequently amended and full of cross-references,' said the brief. It envisioned fourteen separate projects, some of them very large, to be completed under the umbrella of the overall strategy over ten to fifteen years.

Andersen at this stage would have no involvement in the technical implementation of any of the projects – most of that work, farmed out by the Department, had gone to CSC and to other consultants. Andersen, however, would have the key role of advising on the design of the overall architecture of the system, which would have to be common to each one of the fourteen projects in the strategy: different systems of hardware from different suppliers would have to be brought together in a single large-scale network – and they would have to operate reliably. At the same time, the major on-line data bases and the linked applications systems would have to be developed and fitted into a huge open systems network.

The Andersen file copy of the DHSS brief, heavily underlined and scrawled over, shows how closely Burgess went over it. He wrote '14 projects' in the margin against one paragraph, and underlined the word 'senior' four times where the brief insisted that 'the chosen company will be expected to provide a mixed team of senior consultants'. Otway and Burgess himself, each with thirteen years' experience, were as senior as anyone in the business.

In a sense the Department had now embarked on what was to become the classic Whitehall solution to a problem the civil servants could not solve themselves: bring in a director with outside experience (not yet found), and hire a firm of consultants to help him do what the civil servants could not do themselves. As the Thatcher years wore on, there would be dozens of such 'solutions' in every area of government, but this was still early days and of all the departments in government, the DHSS was probably the most hide-bound (although there was some competition for this honour, notably from the Home Office). In that sense it was pioneering stuff, but the officials were very tentative as they stepped suspiciously into the outside world.

For their part, Andersen also had a wider brief which Burgess did not immediately disclose: the firm, like others, was aware of the huge contracts that would become available all over Whitehall over the next decade as the whole of government, and not just the DHSS, automated its operations. The Thatcher government was demanding cost savings and greater efficiency, and computerisation was the best – indeed the only – method of delivering it. But like the DHSS, most of the government departments were horrified at the thought of 'privatising' the design and implementation of computer systems, much preferring to use their own resources, even if that meant taking longer and spending more in the long run. Andersen was in the business, not just of helping the DHSS solve its problems, but also of changing the climate of the whole debate, of persuading the senior officials that outside consultants in general (and not just Andersen) could give them cost and time savings on a scale they could never achieve themselves. If that breakthrough could be made, then the flow of business would increase markedly – and Andersen would be in a position to attract its fair share.

These thoughts, however, were more theoretical than real as, in the middle of January 1983, Burgess and Otway arrived at the Department with a team of three to begin work. Otway (later the head of Andersen's Business Operations Management Group) would be responsible for designing and developing the technical architecture for the whole computer network, an area where Burgess had little expertise. Burgess would oversee the programme management side. Working with them were Chris Davies, Mike Bissett and Chris Turk, all of them men of different talents and backgrounds (Turk, for instance, was an engineer), who were each assigned specific parts of the task.

The Andersen men, even those who had worked in Whitehall before, were at first slightly bemused by the civil servants they encountered in these first few days. They would find them of a higher intellectual calibre than the middle managers they came across in most businesses, but they also found them less motivated. 'There wasn't very much of a "can-do" attitude, which we were used to,' says an Andersen man. The consultants were usually first in and last to leave, grabbing a sandwich at their desk at lunchtime, working through weekends to get a particular report finished, and generally driving themselves in a way quite foreign to most of the career civil servants. Later, as the momentum built up, and particularly after Eric Caines took over in 1987 and civil servants with a computer background, such as Martin Bankier and Phil Dunn, came to drive key parts of the operation, that would change, with civil servants and consultants becoming indistinguishable in their working habits. But for now there was a marked difference, which created a degree of tension and wariness on both sides.

Nor did the condition of the offices in which the operation would be run help. Otway for one remembers a sinking feeling as he arrived at Ray House in Holborn where MSC6, the Civil Service group that had loose overall responsibility for the strategy, was based, to start work on that first Monday morning in mid-January. 'I felt very uncertain about working in government, and then the office was so dingy that I began to think: do I really want to spend three years of my life here? And in those first few weeks and months as we began to throw out ideas there were an awful lot of negative waves. The problem was certainly big and interesting, but the circumstances in which we were working were anything but exciting.'

Otway was probably the only other member of the team who could grasp, at this early stage, the scale and difficulties – and the potential – of the project. It was, he saw clearly, going to be far bigger than even Burgess, who was already thinking in large numbers, realised. Otway had studied the huge and lucrative contract which a similar consultancy with the Inland Revenue had turned into (for CSC). 'I can remember thinking at the time, why didn't we do that? Because it was another one of those big on-line systems, simpler than the Operational Strategy one, but similar,' says Otway. 'So both Keith and I had a sense there was a huge opportunity here.'

There was an air of considerable excitement in the early months, but over it lay a considerable air of nervousness too, on the part of both the consultants and the civil servants. Burgess would later talk about the project being 'very visionary', adding more cautiously: 'but visions are, in themselves, frightening. People can be excited by them, but they can also feel very threatened by what it's going to mean to them to achieve that vision.' At this stage, Otton and Clarke had undoubtedly seen the vision, and were committed to making it happen, but many of the others – including some of the consultants – were nervous.

There were other problems: Burgess soon came to regret strongly the fact that Andersen had not got the Local Office Project at Reading under its control. The overall Operational Strategy included LOP, which had been, as one Andersen man remarked, 'sort of subsumed into it'. But in a fully integrated system, delivering information on the various different benefits through an open systems network onto local office terminals, LOP was the centrepiece of the whole computerisation of the social security system, without which the rest was meaningless. 'So you had this faulty jewel in the crown that you had inherited on terms which you wouldn't have wanted, with power structures already enshrined in the organisation, and somehow you had to subsume it all ...' says the Andersen man. 'At the same time your power to influence the detail of what was being done and who was doing it was very constrained. And civil servants thought the way to manage was to send advisers to fight against each other, which is not my idea of a proper consultancy.'

That, however, would emerge later. In these early months, the main activity for the Andersen team was to put together a highly detailed management plan, which would provide a blueprint for the way the whole project would work. The plan provides an interesting lesson in the way consultants such as Andersen set about solving problems of this kind. Otton and Clarke, looking down on it all from the top of the Department, could only see a project so huge that they did not know where to begin to put it into effect. Burgess took a very straightforward approach: the management plan would break the overall strategy down into manageable, stand-alone parts, cost each bit out, set a time scale for it, assign a team to it – and eventually implement it within the overall structure of the strategy. Each project, of course, would have to be inter-related, and the tricky bit was to ensure there would be no duplication or incompatibility. In a sense, it was much the same practical method used by a contractor building a major bridge, or putting up a multi-floor building – yet it was a way of going about things foreign to most government ministries.

In retrospect, this sounds simple common sense, but at the time it was a considerable leap. 'We have to define an enterprise-wide view – an enterprise architecture, so that each component, when built, will be able to take its place in the jigsaw,' Burgess told his team of consultants and civil servants.

The architecture, he added, would have to allow for changes over time, 'because what you might want to do is to take one component out and replace it with new technology, but you can't let the whole system fall down if that is happening. We have to have a concept which will allow replaceable bricks.'

Nothing quite like it had been done before, and certainly not in the way Burgess was envisioning. 'It was a very creative concept,' said one of the Andersen team years later, 'and it was a major first. People had thought in terms of individual projects, but taking a view across the enterprise was novel.'

Burgess set a rule from these early days which was to prove important for the way the work developed: 'We have to make sure,' he told his team, 'that, should one project end up in serious trouble – slippages or technical problems – it won't delay the whole programme.' He developed his jigsaw analogy, with the pieces fitting together to form an overall picture, but with each individual piece capable of standing alone.

Even when the officials had become persuaded of this, they had to fight battles with the Treasury over this aspect of the strategy. 'One of the things we always suffered from was the original perception that the Operational Strategy was a single project, and I never tired of saying to the Public Accounts Committee and to the Treasury that you cannot have twenty years and nearly £1 billion worth of costs on a single project – that is not manageable,' said one of the officials later.

In April, Burgess brought in a second wave of Andersen people, including the man who, after himself and Otway, would have most input from Andersen into the project. Dave Clinton was in many ways the typical Andersen professional: then only twenty-eight, he was a graduate of Exeter University, had spent three years working on a PhD (on Indian independence) at Oxford but never finished, and joined Andersen in 1979. 'Once you join this firm you live and breathe it,' he said later. He joined at a time when Andersen was committing more and more resources to technology and technology training all over the world. Like every other Andersen recruit, he did his periods of intensive training at St Charles University, and by the early 1980s was cutting his teeth on some of the major Andersen contracts of the time. He would develop into the firm's leading expert in London on 'change management', precisely the discipline that was so lacking in the Department and which could only be introduced from outside.

In the spring of 1983, Clinton was working in the office of an Andersen client when Burgess appeared. He had just finished lunch in the office canteen, and was standing in the corridor chatting to some colleagues when the burly figure of the Welshman stopped in front of him. Burgess outlined the project he wanted him to work on next. The DHSS Operational Strategy, he said, was the biggest thing around in terms of business computing – the biggest in Europe, probably the biggest Andersen had ever tackled worldwide. 'He got me very excited by the sheer scale of the thing. I don't think any of the others had made any sense of it until then.'

Within a few days he had joined the growing Andersen team at Ray House, where they were well into writing the management plan. He arrived as the team were hotly debating the shape it should take: how many centres should there be? Where should they start? 'We need some early results,' Burgess kept saying. 'We must be able to deliver something quickly and show that it can be done and that it works.' What should be the overall architecture? 'It was much like designing a building,' says Clinton. Should they be using IBM or ICL mainframe computers? – an argument that would go all the way to the Cabinet.

It is important at this stage to understand something of the way consultants, particularly Andersen, work on major projects of this kind. Although Burgess was clearly the leader on the team, Otway, as another partner, was very much his peer, working with him rather than for him. Each consultant had his own individual job to do, which would be co-ordinated by Burgess – who was soon to run an entire Andersen division, and after the first year reduced the time he spent on the Operational Strategy to three or four days a week. Clinton and the others might have been junior, but in consulting houses that does not make you subservient – and Clinton is a person who by nature could never kowtow to anyone, even the blunt, forceful

Burgess. In Andersen every decision, every action, has to be justified and argued out before a group of fellow consultants ready to note – and pounce on – the slightest logical error.

In addition, every six months or so, Andersen, as it normally does on large projects, carried out what it calls a 'quality assurance' assessment, whereby a senior consultant not involved with the project analyses the work done by his colleagues. The audit in this case was done by Larry R. Levitan who flew in from the US to review the work. At the end of each 'QA' there would be dinner. In this case, Levitan had dinner with Geoffrey Otton and Norman Clarke. Martin Vandersteen, Andersen's senior partner and Burgess's overall boss, would also attend – as of course would Burgess. They were tough, working sessions, at which Levitan would listen and voice his opinion of the project so far, and they would discuss their strategic concerns. 'It was useful to get a different insight on the way things were progressing,' says Clarke. 'I would come away from a meeting like that with three or four points in my mind that I would want to follow up. And Geoffrey would have another three or four which he would ask me to follow up.'

By the summer, there were nine Andersen people at work on the project, still only a fraction of the numbers it would eventually grow to, and they were putting the finishing touches to the management plan. Mark Otway was well advanced on designing the overall architecture – 'what sort of shape should the system be, how should the different projects fit together, how should we build them, how do you organise yourself on the project and so on'; Chris Davies had drawn up an outline for the application and data side; while Clinton was well down the road on his analysis of the best way of transferring millions of files, many of which were incomplete and inaccurate, onto the new computer data base.

'Basically all consulting work can be distilled down to three phases, no matter how you dress it up,' says Clinton. 'There is fact-finding or data-gathering; the analytical phase which usually comes up with the options; and there is a report-production and presentation phase.' They were now at the fact-finding stage.

During the summer of 1983, the team of consultants and civil servants began to slot together, friendships developing as the Andersen people came to respect the officials and the officials began to drop their resentment of these outsiders brought in to tell them what to do. Burgess and John Ray, the technical head of the unit in Ray House, developed a friendship that would last longer than the project.

At this stage, the project was ill defined, and even the consultants often found it difficult to see the direction in which they wanted to go.

'In the very early days there was a lot of thrashing about,' says one Andersen man, 'with nobody really knowing what they were doing. Civil servants would come down from Newcastle or whatever, playing a role rather than contributing very much – it was all done in an ivory tower. A lot of the work was unreal, and could never have been implemented properly. We spent months on data analysis – hours and hours, days and weeks, thrashing around. It was still largely theoretical, and it was only later that people started getting practical.'

Otway spent the first six months working out the architecture of a system to handle an operation which had so far defied all the experts. By any standards this was a major intellectual exercise. He had few yardsticks, because the geographical, functional and technical sides of the operation were all beyond the boundaries of any established architecture. He had to take a new and innovative approach, pioneering his own methodologies and techniques. Basically, he would have to lay down the architecture of a system capable of supporting a flow of data to and from over seventy mainframe computers in at least six locations scattered over Britain (four area computer centres plus two central facilities). Up to 26,000 terminals in the local offices must be able to feed into the mainframes, and be capable of producing up-to-date details for each claimant across the whole range of benefits – the 'whole person' approach. The hardware used on the separate projects would inevitably be different, so his architecture would have to accommodate that too, and be integrated with the nationwide communications network, which would have to allow clerks anywhere in the country access to all the different benefit systems.

As he worked on his blueprint, Otway was also conscious of something else: not only must he get all the pieces – data, functions, applications, protocols, operating systems, hardware and communications systems – to fit together, he also had to produce an architecture robust enough to allow for major additions over the next ten years. It was clear, as Burgess had said from the start, that hardware would be added to, taken off, upgraded – and there would be new benefits and other additions to cope with. Whatever the pressures and the changes, the network would have to remain up and running. He therefore had to lay down common standards and a plan that could be achieved progressively – Otway improved on Burgess's analogy by talking about a 'three dimensional' jigsaw, the third dimension being time. Integration on such a massive scale required a unique technical architecture, which was beyond the range of the civil servants and which would tax Otway and his team (including the best of the civil servants) to the limit.

By July, Otway had put his initial thoughts down in a paper that would become ANNEXE 4 of the management plan, a detailed, technical and precise proposal for making the system work. This was the heart of the Andersen plan, which would set the course for the next decade and beyond. There would, he wrote, be 'technical firsts' in the four main components of the technical infrastructure he was designing: a central index containing details of almost everyone in Britain; the branch office systems which had so far eluded all attempts to mechanise; a countrywide open systems interconnect (OSI) network; and four major data centres with the big ICL mainframes in different parts of the country.

Otway's 'architecture' was of course just that – a blueprint for a system that still had to be designed, developed, built, tested and installed. It would need hundreds of skilled civil servants and consultants to write the programmes that would make it work, and thousands more to install and implement it. Most of the software for the DHSS's Operational Strategy would be written by its own civil servants, with the help of Andersen and specialist outside suppliers. Andersen, with its experience of designing such systems, could anticipate the pits into which the civil servants had fallen in the past, and then, later, work out a detailed plan on how the systems should be put in place, with all that meant for training, redesigning unsuitable offices to take it, and all the rest of it. It would require, as an Andersen brief said later, 'a programme the size and complexity of which made it one of the largest civil computerisation programmes yet conducted anywhere.'

In the summer of 1983, as he finished his piece of the report, Otway was in no doubt about the magnitude of the task – and of the risks involved for Andersen, which was already becoming critical to the project. But he, and Burgess, were confident it could be done.

By the autumn of 1983, it was also clear to Burgess that he needed more consultants on the job. The more the Andersen people examined it, the more they realised this was something far, far bigger than they – or anyone else – had envisaged. People had grasped the scale of the problem; they had not understood the scale of the solution which was going to be far more costly than they had planned for. Even with its enlarged team, the Andersen consultants were spread very thinly, and the pace they could run at was entirely dependent on the quality of the civil servants they were working with. With a number of exceptions, this was not, on the whole, very high – the Department possessed too few people trained in the skills needed. That also had to be factored into the plan.

The management plan was finished by August and pulled together by Otway. Clinton contributed a couple of chapters, Otway's technical architecture section was bound in, and Burgess then took it away for a weekend. He appeared bleary-eyed on the Monday morning with twenty-five pages of management summary. It was an extraordinarily detailed document, not intended to be read at a single sitting. Its different chapter headings and sections set out the framework for the different aspects of the project: here was a step-by-step plan that would become the Bible for the Operational Strategy from now on. It would stand the test of time remarkably well.

Until that time, Otton, Clarke, and some of the Department's seasoned and best technology people had seen the vision, but had only the vaguest of ideas about how it would be translated into practice. Burgess broke the plan down into what he called the 'Ten Commandments', and put them on a slide. Presented that way, they appeared fairly simple, straightforward – and 'do-able'. The first commandment was that the project must be tackled in phases and not as one single exercise; then the data would have to be managed; a technical infrastructure would have to be built along the lines Otway had set out; there must be common working methods; Clarke's 'Sausages' committee should become a full Operational Strategy steering committee, which would oversee it; MSC6 should become a directorate, with a degree of autonomy and complete control over the whole operation, particularly the Local Office Project (LOP); and so on.

He presented this to Norman Clarke's committee, and to Otton, who, from his office at the top of Alexander Fleming House at the Elephant and Castle, was pushing it forward with all the enthusiasm a permanent secretary was capable of. Burgess had been around Whitehall long enough to know how difficult it was to get something like this accepted, and this was to be no exception. Clarke quickly agreed that the management plan was 'about right' and was pointing in the right direction, but there were two or three further meetings, while Burgess took the committee through all the areas of the plan in detail. That was followed by a long debate over several months before the senior civil servants finally accepted it.

Burgess trotted from office to office, explaining it with slides and flip-charts, trying to show the way the targets could be met. 'The management plan is all about making the vision achievable,' he expounded. 'It's about breaking the work down into a series of small tasks, about preparing a base line for the work that needs to be executed.' To his colleagues, he explained the need to persuade the officials, still bruised from their former experiences and not really believing the consultants could do any better, that it could be done, and the way to do it was to set out the activities which could then 'be ticked off on a board' as they were tackled.

As the year wore on, it was becoming more and more apparent that the figure of £700 million allotted to the project was a gross underestimate, essentially because it was growing and being added to. At the other end of the costing, it was also becoming apparent that the proposed savings, at least for the rest of the 1980s, were also an exaggeration. The gap between expenditure and saving was narrowing all the time as the Andersen men laid out the bones of the management plan that would govern the project for the next decade. In Reading, perhaps predictably, the Local Office Project was running both above budget and well behind schedule, headed for yet further major problems.

By the autumn of 1983, Burgess had over twenty Andersen men working at the DHSS, with the numbers still rising. By that stage he was already arguing that not only was the budgeted figure for the overall project hopelessly inadequate, but much more would have to be spent on consultants. He delivered that message at a meeting with John Ray and John Handby, and to their immediate boss Mike Fogden (now a Grade III civil servant, the head of the Employment Service, and one of the programmers who successfully made the leap into senior management). If they were surprised, they should not have been by then. In consultancy jobs, it is a fairly normal occurrence that a small job grows into a bigger one, and indeed the consultants are trained to encourage it to do so. Most clients, and the DHSS was no exception here, start with a limited concept of what they want from the consultants. Once the consultants are in, they quickly discover that there is no real point in tackling a limited area of work – each task within an organisation relates to another, and unless the client is willing to change large sections of the organisation there is little purpose in tackling one small part.

Implementing the Operational Strategy had implications for the whole of the way the DHSS delivered its benefits, and would directly affect the working habits of over 100,000 people who worked for it. Inevitably, if Andersen did its job properly, the contract would broaden and lengthen. Burgess had banked on that when he went for the job, sensing the limited contract

Andersen was offered initially would not last the year. And he was right. By the end of 1983, there were over thirty Andersen people involved in some of the individual projects contained within the Operational Strategy.

By that stage, however, there were frustrations too. The planning period seemed to be lasting interminably, with no action as yet. Tempers sometimes frayed, and the new Andersen people did not always mesh in as well as the older ones. At one stage, Burgess called all the Andersen people to a meeting in the basement of Ray House and began his lecture: 'You're not drinking enough!' As they stared at him, astonished, he went on to expound the need to get closer to the civil servants. The Andersen people were coming in early, working late, and going home. From now on, he insisted, they must spend more time in the pub, the Cartoonist or the famous White Hart (known for years as 'The Stab in the Back' after the Mirror journalists who drank there), chatting with the civil servants. The Andersen people willingly complied.

The whole project, however, still lacked momentum. What it needed, Burgess decided, was 'a victory', however small – a project which they could crack on with, get under their belt, and thereby improve everyone's morale.

Fortunately, there was one readily available: it would be many years before the local offices could get their on-line system up and running, but there was nothing to stop them moving quickly to ordinary micro-computers, which would be well short of what was required – they would have no access to a central data base – but would have a number of benefits. This was essentially the short-term solution urged on Clarke several years before by Logica, and Andersen, in its role as adviser to the overall strategy, was not against it – albeit with some reservations. Modern electronic technology was almost totally unknown in the local offices, so micro-computers would pave the way for the more complex systems which would come later. They would also improve morale and speed up the process of claims.

Otton and Mike Fogden took the micro-computer plan, which they called LOMP, to the Treasury, which approved it, but insisted, in line with the new Thatcher doctrine, that it went out to competitive tender. The consultants were far from happy with that, basically because they were not convinced they would get the machines they wanted, which were IBM-compatibles. By now the Andersen team was becoming familiar with the odd rules of procurement which all government departments practised in the 1984–5 period (later they would change as lessons were learned and the system became more sophisticated). But they were still easily baffled by them, and never more so than when it came to procuring the micro-computers – some 2,500 terminals which would go into the local offices. Otway and his team had a very clear idea of what was required, and sat down to write the 'operational requirement' in the request proposal, which they hoped would provide the micro-computers he wanted. As he completed the necessary full study report required by the Treasury before they even went out to tender, Otway laid down the list of 'mandatories' – the functions the machines would have to be capable of undertaking even to be considered for the job – after which he added the list of 'desirables', which were extra features he would like the machines to have. Under the system, he knew that the CCTA, the part of the Treasury that oversees all government computer purchases, would then arrive at a short-list of machines – a minimum of three – which would be required to demonstrate that they could meet the mandatories. Once this had been agreed, the short-listed suppliers would get a detailed memorandum of understanding, on the basis of which they would price and send in their bid.

As usual, the bids in this case would not be sent in to the DHSS or Andersen, but to the CCTA, which would make its usual adjustment to the price to allow for the 'desirables' offered by the different suppliers. But at the end of the day, whoever put in the lowest bid would win.

'You had to be very thorough at the front end of that process to avoid getting anyone on that short-list that has no hope of doing the job,' says an Andersen man. 'And that was a very difficult intellectual exercise. It was all done in very logical, requirement terms, which if you weren't very careful would deliver totally the wrong hardware or software. We kept hitting problems such as someone saying "we're designing systems that need keyboards with function keys on them", and we would think you could tell the suppliers what the keyboard should look like. But the CCTA would say, "No, you can't tell them what the keyboard will look like – what you can say is that there is a requirement for a function key", and you would then have to describe what a function key looked like. It was really Byzantine.'

Andersen and the teams they worked with spent many long hours in the 1984–5 period fighting to ensure that they ended up with systems that would eventually inter-link and could deliver the 'whole person' concept on a single terminal.

In the case of the LOMP micro-computer, Otway was not allowed to say, as he wanted, 'This computer must be able to run MS-DOS', because under the Treasury rules that would have been deemed unfair to other systems. He thought long and hard about it, and ingeniously – or so he thought – came up with a phrase he thought would get around that. 'The machines must be able to run a leading, popular micro-computer operating system,' he wrote, reckoning that could only be MS-DOS. He could not have been more wrong. What they ended up with were machines able to run Concurrent CPM, a system that just about qualified as 'leading and popular' but which was already a generation old and disappeared from the market soon afterwards. 'So long as they could say "tick" to the question, "Does it run a leading, popular micro-computer operating system?", you can't then say, we won't have them,' says Otway.

Thus the Department ended up with Logica machines, which were not IBM-compatible 16-bit machines, but 8-bit micros. They were cheap, but they were also, as one Andersen man remarked acerbically, old-fashioned technology, 'boxes that are not going anywhere'. A year into the project, Logica pulled out of the PC market, rubbing home the point.

But as they began to install them in the offices, there were other problems which no one had foreseen – not the manufacturers, the Department's experts, or even Andersen. In the Crystal Palace area of South London, for instance, the machines suddenly began to throw out gobbledygook, making wild miscalculations which for weeks no one could explain. Finally, someone, looking up at the two huge television masts that broadcast both BBC and independent television to south-east England, worked it out: the wires connecting up the different PCs in the local offices, which were now handling Geoffrey Otton's bar-coding breakthrough, were acting as a giant aerial, picking up the television signal. In other offices, never designed for computers, there were problems from underfloor heating, from faulty wiring, and so on. It was not the fault of the computers – it was simply inexperience in trying to weld such a system together.

Andersen only had a peripheral involvement in the project, trying to see it as a part of the overall strategy rather than as a stand-alone project (which is essentially what it was), but as the problems arose, Burgess threw in some more of his men to help get it working. The project did bring to the fore a man who was to turn into one of the stars of the strategy over the next few years: Phil Dunn joined the DHSS straight from school, and spent the first three years of his career working in a social security local office. He had been an early adherent of computers, however, and developed his skills as a programmer at Reading. He took time out to do consultancy work in Saudi Arabia and a tour as a course director at the Civil Service College, where he passed on his computer expertise. A rounded, balding, genial man, then in his forties, he soon put his stamp on the micro project, and in its limited way it began to work – the first modest step along the road to implementing the Operational Strategy which by that stage was already six years old. It was also the success that established Dunn, later to play a key role in the strategy, as probably the best trouble-shooter in the Department, and a man the Andersen people came to have a considerable respect for.

LOMP was also the first real test of one of the elements of the Andersen strategy – one which Dunn was also a fan of. 'The way we found was most effective in delivering the many projects within the overall programme,' he said later, 'was to break them down into a mind-boggling level of detail at which you could be sure that a small group of people – five people, say, for two weeks – had a discrete unit of work, which was visible. Therefore you could be clear, very early on, whether that unit, which ultimately was a small part of a very much bigger picture, was being delivered not only to time but was being delivered with the requisite quality.' This, he adds, was particularly good for morale 'because of the possibility of achieving early success – the fact that a milestone, a target, had been met.'

'Tactically, LOMP, whatever its inadequacies, was always worth underwriting,' said Burgess later. 'It was the first building block in getting things forward, because it meant putting technology out into all these offices, and letting people have a feel for things. It actually provided the foundation for the big roll-out operation of 1989–90.'

All of that, although it took Andersen more than three years of project time, was a sideshow, peripheral to the main task of the strategy. Beside it ran another sideshow, albeit one that was big enough to constitute a major operation in its own right. There was another bit of technology which could be introduced relatively easily: an improvement and updating of the unemployment benefit system. This project was known in DHSS parlance as Terminal Replacement/Enquiry Service, or TRES, and was to be another modest step forward. The unemployment offices around the country were at that point operating on a system designed in the 1960s and installed in the 1970s, using a terminal that was basically a device that looked – and sounded – like an old-fashioned teletype, chattering out its information all day long. Andersen had not been in the job long before it became apparent to everyone that unless the old teletype machines were replaced quickly the whole system of unemployment benefit would come crashing down. 'These things had been in there ten years and basically they had chattered themselves to death,' remarked a consultant afterwards.

Their replacement eventually involved putting some 1000 Honeywell DPS6 mini-computers and 10,000 terminals into the unemployment benefit offices all over the country. The

Andersen people saw this as a good solution – the Honeywell, unlike the Logica machine, was suitable for the job, although relatively expensive. But again they watched in some bafflement the process through which they were acquired. The Employment Service, which would operate them, insisted on putting into the business requirement, which went to the Treasury's CCTA where it was accepted, that there could only be twenty-four terminals per machine. 'There was no logic to it whatsoever,' says an Andersen man. 'They just came up with this twenty-four maximum figure – and hence you get Honeywell. If they'd said "unlimited", they'd probably have got British Telecom or something else. But they put in the twenty-four and that meant Honeywell and it turned out to be a good solution. But it was procurement nonsense.'

Information could be inputted onto the Honeywells in the offices, and they could be networked, communicating through British Telecom's package-switching network to the NUBS ICL mainframes in Reading and Livingston. The problems here were not the system itself – that proved reasonably straightforward – but the communications network, many of the components of which were new and untested.

What should have been another easy 'victory' chalked up for the strategy began, like so many other projects before it, to go wrong. The TRES system as envisaged by the Department, with a minimal input from Andersen, was a badly thought-out plan, basically taking the 1960s system and updating it, rather than making use of the changes in technology over the period. What emerged was a mixture of 1980s and 1960s technology (unemployment would only become part of the on-line strategy system in the 1990s, with the completion of the more advanced project, NUBS 2).

Burgess bounced these problems off Levitan when the American appeared on his six-monthly 'jumbo job' quality-assurance review. 'The risk is that while the client looks to us for the success of the project, we do not have sufficient involvement in all of the major areas to control at any level of detail the quality of work and the development status,' wrote

Burgess in one of his quality-assurance reports to Levitan. Levitan agreed, pointing out that, according to the normal Andersen rules, the firm should have much more control of such a high-risk project. On the other hand, from what he could see of it, it was working, so there was no reason not to continue.

Andersen had doubts about the way the Department wanted to do TRES, but in the end was persuaded by the civil servants of the course they had chosen. Burgess threw in nine Andersen people to buttress the team, and to help with some of the key risk control. By the end of 1986, TRES was working, hitting its original 95% reliability target, by which stage the team was being asked for more. Burgess remained cautious about it, though. 'This project may represent the case where we have enough participation to take the blame but not enough participation to actually fix anything,' he wrote in his quality-assurance report in December 1986. But, he added, 'at this point ... no fingers are being pointed at us.'

The micro-computer project and the updated unemployment system, however, were almost distractions from the main task Andersen had been set. The concept of the 'whole person' treatment could only be achieved with a vast inter-linked network, a central index, and terminals at the local offices. Progress on those fronts was not going so well.

CHAPTER FOUR

The NEW DIRECTOR

Before Andersen ever appeared on the scene, Otton and Clarke had decided that the DHSS Operational Strategy needed its own director. It had become the fashion in Whitehall to look outside for directors for large projects: the Ministry of Defence had brought in an outsider to oversee weapons procurement, and there were outsiders now in health, trade and industry and other departments. The idea of giving the DHSS its own high-powered strategy director had been arrived at early in 1982, and was intended to be a central part of the plan set out in the Green Paper. In the event, it was put on hold while the Green Paper was published and absorbed, and held still further while the officials went about hiring consultants.

Andersen supported the view that MSC6 should be turned into a directorate, which obviously meant having a director to run it, but through 1983, although there was some talk about it, nothing was done about getting in the man the Department wanted. With the completion of the management plan, however, it became a priority. At first, however, the Department looked inside rather than outside for its man. There was a good reason for this: it happened to have in its ranks a man with as much drive and ability as it was likely ever to find in the private sector. Eric Caines had been involved with the strategy from the beginning, a member of Clarke's 'group grope' with strong opinions vigorously voiced and defended, and therefore had been involved with drafting the template of the strategy. It was Caines who, as much as anyone else in the Department, had been responsible for scuppering CAMELOT, and it was he, certainly as much as anyone else, who had tried to take on board its principal lessons.

Because of CAMELOT and so many other public failures, the word around Whitehall by this stage was that the least enviable job in the world was to be director of the Operational Strategy at the DHSS. 'People were running a mile at the thought of it,' says one official. The Department, towards the end of 1983, began to advertise the job, but Geoffrey Otton had another idea. One day he took Caines aside, and suggested that he should apply – with the clear implication that he would get it. Clarke would be retiring within a few years, and Otton, who would also have gone by then, hoped that Caines would take over from him and see the strategy through to its end.

Caines reluctantly agreed to apply. He was easily the most serious applicant – until out of the blue another man threw his hat into the ring.

Brigadier John William Charles Spackman was born in 1932, the son of an army colonel, and had served in the forces for thirty years. He was an unusual soldier, in that his interests from the early days had been academic and technical; he was a boffin, a man fascinated by the application of electronic technology to the modern army. When the British Army moved to state-of-the-art operational research techniques in the early 1970s, Spackman, by then in possession of a battery of academic qualifications including a first-class honours degree, a PhD and an MSc in management science, became the leader of the systems analysis team which designed them. He had been the chief military officer at the Ministry of Defence's chemical warfare plant at Porton Down, the senior designer of Project Wavell, which was a complex mobile field-commander unit, and finally ended up as director of the Army's Supply Computer Services. His computer systems played a vital role in the Falklands War, with Spackman in charge of the support operation in Britain and Germany; he even set up an electronic mail system which worked perfectly between headquarters in Britain and the troops in the Falklands.

However, at the end of the war, he decided to quit the Army, basically seeking other fields. He was tempted by an offer from the China Power and Light company in Hong Kong, and was headed there when an advertisement in the Sunday Times caught his eye. He applied for the job of director of the DHSS's Operational Strategy.

To some of the senior officials, irritated by Caines's abrasiveness, Spackman's application was a godsend. Because he already had his army pension, the brigadier was not deterred, as other serious outside candidates were, by the (relatively) low pay the job offered. He was also intrigued by the concept of the strategy, particularly as it related to computers. 'What I liked about it was its obvious emphasis on strategic networking,' he said later. 'All too often computer projects are considered in isolation, and this was what had happened in the past in social security: there was a pensions system, and there was the National Insurance Recording System, and a child benefit system, each one independently automated, with no concept of the fact that the person you're serving, the public, is an individual or a family group. This cross-functional integration and networking of computer systems had always interested me.'

Spackman read Patrick Jenkin's 1980 working paper before he went along to be interviewed by Norman Clarke and other officials, and was excited by it. 'I thought it was super stuff, a really first-class document. It was pretty thin technically, but in business and operational terms, and in terms of strategic thinking, I thought it was very advanced.'

At the interview he was as impressed by Clarke as Clarke was by him. Clarke, recalls Spackman, was 'very tough' but also practical, with a clear view of what he wanted to do. 'He put great emphasis on control remaining with the users, and was very much afraid of the technology driving the Department.' Spackman instantly agreed, saying that he believed the user had to be in the driving seat. 'I couldn't go forward with a project like this unless it is under constant user strategic direction,' he told Clarke. 'It needs a strong and active user steering committee, because usually the problem is that the users say, well, this is what we want in terms of computerisation and then they back away from the project until it's delivered, and then they say, this isn't really what I wanted.' He was adamant that if he were to take the job the users – which really meant the local offices who had to deal with the public – had to be involved 'both in the direction of the system, and actively in the functional design, all the way through.'

The user had of course been involved in CAMELOT, and that had not helped the project, but much had changed since then, not least the fact that there was now an overall Operational Strategy governing – at least in theory, although not yet in practice – the mechanisation of the welfare system. Nonetheless, as Otton was nervously aware, there was nothing magic about designing the system from the users' end. By that stage there were many senior officials seriously doubting whether an integrated system could be achieved at all.

But the point is that from the outset Clarke and Spackman saw eye to eye, with Otton above them supporting them with all the restrained enthusiasm he was capable of. Caines, having been persuaded against his better judgement to take on the job – he even went for the interview – now found himself rejected. He was still director of the regional operation, one of the biggest jobs in the social security system, and a member of Clarke's steering committee, but the Whitehall machine found something almost as challenging for him. He went to the Home Office to take on the considerable task of bringing change to Britain's prison system. But he left with his criticism of the way the whole operation was being run undiluted. 'The thing was dragging on interminably. People were beginning to say: "You've offered us glimpses of this bold new world, but here we are still beleaguered in our offices, working quill-pen-style, swamped in paper, and we're not seeing anything for all this great talk in Whitehall." And they wanted to see something happening. We were going into greater and greater refinements, drawing up functional analyses of the way things ought to relate, how we should run it, but getting into all sorts of supply problems, who's going to be providing the equipment at different stages of this thing, who provides the terminals, who provides the mainframes, what's your communication system in the middle, are they going to be compatible and so on. I mean endless, endless, debate on these things. And by the time I went to the Home Office to do the prison thing in 1984, people were beginning to believe that this would never appear, saying "This is talk, this has been going on for almost a decade now." '

Spackman was offered the job, immediately accepted it, and began work early in 1984. His office was in the same miserable building, just behind the Daily Mirror building, as the

Andersen people occupied, later made all the more intolerable by the frequent comings and goings of Robert Maxwell's helicopter. 'I couldn't believe the office when I saw it,' said Spackman. 'It was a sort of old benefits building which was at the lower end of the scale of elegance in government buildings – and when you consider the headquarters in Alexander Fleming House, that really was saying something!'

Once he was over the initial shock, however, Spackman didn't mind, immersing himself in the task in hand. That task, he soon became aware, was an even bigger one than he had imagined. Essentially, he was now in charge of all the different, incompatible computer systems within the Department, scattered from Newcastle to North Fylde and Reading, and little had yet been done about bringing them under a single control. This meant drawing directly into the strategy the computerisation of short-term benefit, which the people at Reading were now making heavy weather of.

Spackman inherited a team in place in Ray House, supplemented by over thirty Andersen people. He also took operational control of the other teams in Newcastle and elsewhere, but these he would leave in place.

As he travelled the country, Spackman was impressed by some of the systems already running. Whatever their faults of inflexibility, the Newcastle systems did what they were supposed to with impressive efficiency – recording millions of contributions and paying out billions of pounds in pensions. 'The pensions system and the national insurance system, both of them huge systems, were actually very competently put together, but they were old-fashioned in their architecture.' That, he adds, is 'not a comment on the people who did it, it was the time they were built'.

But if he had been surprised by the lack of strategy for the different systems when he went up for his interview, he was now shaken by it. In terms of understanding networking, he said later, the DHSS was years behind the Ministry of Defence, and hopelessly old-fashioned in comparison to what the banks, building societies and airlines were already doing.

'There was absolutely no strategy, no consistency of method

or data standards or approach, no concept of how to transfer information between one system and another. And there were a lot of embarrassing incidents as a result, like reminders going out to people who had been dead for years. It was all happening because of the lack of communication between the systems.'

If Otton, Clarke and even the Andersen people reckoned that by this stage, some five or six years since the Operational Strategy had been conceived, they were now going forward, that was not the way Spackman, seeing it as an outsider for the first time, was struck by it. There was, he remarked later, 'absolutely no momentum'. Even after all this time, everything still seemed to be under discussion, with very little action. 'There was no positive plan for implementation, and we had to get a number of things in place. The first was to put in this strong steering structure and a good steering committee which took personal management responsibility for the plan. Secondly, it was necessary to strengthen the business justification to the Treasury, and to convince them it would pay – that was not well structured. Then we had to introduce good, strong project management and software engineering techniques, because again some of the projects were not project managed – they grew, with good technical control but hopeless financial and resources control, and control of time. And then there was the concept of the architecture: if you were going to network things together, you have to start working on defining the architecture of the systems that you are going to build. Finally, there was the recognition that there just wasn't the skill base within the Department, and there was no time to grow it.'

There are, however, differing views of Spackman's contribution by those who worked alongside him. To some he was a hero, bringing direction and momentum to the project. To others he was something else. 'He was as much a barrier to getting momentum going as anyone else,' says one of the team, 'because he basically wanted to debate esoteric data-base distribution issues, when we were trying to say, as long as we've got a system that works and we can implement, we can move forward and get something done.' The Andersen team also insist that it was they who put the steering structure in place, not Spackman

– it was there before he arrived.

Spackman's impressions of the strategy were not improved, however, by the first meeting of Clarke's committee he attended, when the subject of the TRES national unemployment benefit project, halfway through by that stage, came up. At that point it was clearly going wildly wrong, and after listening to the discussion, Spackman shook his head in bewilderment. 'It will never work,' he said. Burgess, however, had now come round to the officials' view that it would, and offered further Andersen people to ensure that it did. Spackman readily agreed.

Yet it was from this point that the Operational Strategy, slowly at first but with a steadily rising momentum, began to get off the ground. It was hard work, with all sorts of obstacles which would probably never have been encountered in the private sector. The Treasury, Spackman found, was profoundly suspicious of his directorate and of the DHSS's strategy, largely because of its past failures at computerising. 'CAMELOT was constantly being raised,' says one official. 'It came up again and again, and I think it was one of the major difficulties and one of the reasons the project was delayed. There was a substantial delay in actually getting started properly because of Treasury caution. It was hard to get project approval.'

This was not entirely the fault of the Treasury. The Thatcher government's attempts to cut expenditure were now at their height, and, as both ministers and civil servants discovered, it was much easier to cut capital expenditure than it was to reduce manpower. The Treasury had long learned the trick of simply deferring approval for capital expenditure into the next financial year, thus relieving the pressure on the short-term public-sector borrowing requirement, but adding to the cost of the project itself. Because capital expenditure had visibly – and publicly – gone astray in the DHSS's forlorn attempts at automation, the Treasury could feel justified in denying it priority now.

From the moment he arrived, Spackman, often flanked by the two senior civil servants in the Department, Ken Stowe, the permanent secretary for the entire DHSS, and Otton, who was the second permanent secretary covering social security, was in almost daily battle with the Treasury. He also inherited something else: another inquiry by the Public Accounts Committee into the costly computerisation programmes of government departments in general. CAMELOT and the DHSS stood out as the big blot on this particular landscape.

The House of Commons, 28 March 1984: Sir Geoffrey Otton filed into a committee room to sit before eleven MPs from the powerful Public Accounts Committee. In the chair was Robert Sheldon, a veteran Labour member with a nose for public waste and a keen eye for suspect accounting practices. With Otton were the most senior officials involved in his Operational Strategy: Clarke, of course, and Spackman, who had just joined. With them were two other high-powered Treasury men: Alan Bailey, second permanent secretary, and Paul Freeman, who was the director of the Treasury's Central Computer and Telecommunications Agency, which had an overall strategic responsibility for all the computerisation programmes across Whitehall, including the Operational Strategy. Sheldon began, courteously but directly, with a question for Bailey.

'On the wider computer issues,' he said, 'the importance of strategic planning has been recognised for many years, since at least 1978. Five years later its adoption is patchy and doesn't measure up to the financial and operational benefits at stake.' He quoted from a recent report from Sir Gordon Downey, the Comptroller and Auditor General (also waiting to give evidence that day), which had been highly critical of the DHSS's automation progress and of CAMELOT in particular. 'Why did it take so long to secure action on this issue that was effective?' asked Sheldon.

Bailey quickly ducked that question, suggesting that Otton could 'expound on the Operational Strategy' at the DHSS later. But he went on to explain that almost all government departments now had strategies for information technology, all of them progressing at different paces. Sheldon concentrated his questions on the shortage of computer skills right through the Civil Service, which was holding implementation back. 'We are putting a lot of effort into more training and attempting ... to get skills in from the outside,' said Bailey. In the case of the DHSS, he said later, 'having established a strategy is not the end of the matter. The problem evolves, and a lot more work has to be done and a certain amount of revision of objectives may have to be undertaken.'

Bailey, however, was not the PAC's main target that day – Otton was. When it came to his turn, Sheldon this time was less courteous. 'Could I start by asking you about the lessons of CAMELOT?' he began, before going on to list the Green Paper's proposed 'fourteen major computer projects over a fifteen-year period at an additional cost of £700 million'. Sheldon paused, then leaned forward. 'Are you satisfied that this ambitious project can be handled by you?'

Otton had been expecting that, and had an answer. The DHSS had been one of the first government departments to produce a strategy, he said. That strategy had not been easy to devise. 'It takes an enormous amount of analysis and work, and we have only got to where we have got to now by starting back in 1977 when we felt the benefit systems had reached a point of equilibrium and the pressures on them were such that we really needed to stand back and see if we could devise a way forward which made coherent sense.' Could the Department now handle it? 'I will be bold and say yes,' said Otton firmly. 'We have recruited Dr Spackman [he indicated the man sitting on his left] who brings a great deal of technical expertise into the Department. We are making very extensive use of consultants. At the moment ... we are on course very safely on the things we are trying.'

Sheldon had a question for Spackman: had anyone ever successfully computerised operations of the scale and complexity the DHSS was trying to tackle?

There were far more complex operations in defence, particularly in the US, Spackman told him. 'What is possibly unique about this one is its size,' he added. 'I do not know of a project that actually involves quite as large a number of on-line terminals.' However, the actual application itself, he said, was not 'leading-edge' or particularly complicated. 'If it were being done on a much smaller system it would indeed be a fairly pedestrian and straightforward project. It is its size which makes it complicated.' That conflicted with what Otway and other experts, particularly those labouring on LOP at Reading, believed: to them the system was very 'leading-edge' indeed – and later, as he came to understand more of the problems, Spackman would probably agree.

As Sheldon turned back to Otton, the second permanent secretary had a nasty surprise for the committee. The Local Office Project was officially expected to cost £200 million and save £380 million, Sheldon said, quoting the published figures from the Green Paper in October 1982. Were these still firm figures?

No, Otton had to reply, they were not. That £380 million had dropped to only £66 million. There was a gasp from the committee. 'That is very disquieting,' Sheldon continued, again bringing up CAMELOT. That was a huge drop. Finally, with a withering 'You must understand that we will obviously be taking a much closer interest in these matters in the light of the comments that you have just made', he turned back to Bailey. But one by one the other members of his committee came back again and again to Otton, still finding it hard to believe the fall in the profitability of LOP. Why should they accept there would even be a saving of £66 million? Where would it come from? How firm was it? Finally, after two highly uncomfortable hours, Otton and his team staggered out. The DHSS's Operational Strategy had not had a good day.

In fact Otton, largely as a result of Spackman, was feeling more confident than he was able to convey to the committee. The original figures in the Green Paper had been highly tentative, based on a staff saving of 6000. That, Spackman and Andersen had worked out, was not going to be achievable. But Spackman was committed to delivering savings of 4000 jobs. He was also making more and more use of Andersen, steadily widening its brief even further.

'Going around meeting people, even in the first few weeks, I determined that there was really no chance whatsoever of doing it quickly with Department resources,' he said later. 'It wasn't a matter of their abilities – they were very good – but their experience and training were not appropriate for the sort of project we were tackling.'

Yet even Spackman was reluctant to take this logic to its obvious conclusion. The Department was committing itself to a very large expenditure programme without the internal expertise to make it work. Several years later, after a lengthy learning curve, the inhibitions would drop away and the officials would have gone straight to the solution which Andersen was already working hard to steer them towards: if you haven't got the people who can do it, hire a team from outside who can, who can then work jointly with the civil servants, passing on to them the necessary expertise. Some time later, when it came to the issue of family credit, Spackman would indeed draw that conclusion, but at this stage the consultants were still having to push very hard to open the door a crack wider. Consultants and officials, however, see Spackman's initiative from different viewpoints, one side feeling that he went too slowly – which he obviously did from their point of view – the other that he was a major innovatory influence.

Andersen and CSC were already working for the Department, but not in the central role which Burgess and Otway were arguing they needed. Over the two years Andersen had been working on the project, their role had subtly altered, but even now the civil servants regarded them with suspicion. Martin Bankier, controller of the North Fylde central office (with a staff of 5000, dealing with a mixture of health and social security using large-batch computer systems), ruefully acknowledges his own doubts at the time. 'There was a bit of a tendency for people like me in North Fylde and my colleague in Newcastle to say, well, we've been doing these computer operations for a long time, but you give us the money to develop on-line systems and we'll jolly well develop it. And John Spackman came along and said, "You've been doing in effect what you've been good at, batch processing systems, for far too long. Really, your level of expertise on current computer systems is too low within the Department. The only way of doing this is to bring in considerable consultancy assistance." And he was absolutely right.'

Bankier was another man who would play an important role in the Operational Strategy, not as central or important as that of Dunn, but critical nonetheless. A traditional, long-term civil servant, Bankier was older than the others, having joined the Inland Revenue as a tax officer immediately after the war. He also had more experience of the Civil Service: in 1950 he moved to the Ministry of Food and then to the Ministry of Pensions (later part of the DHSS) in 1953, where, like Dunn later, he had become a computer buff. He had worked on finance, on pensions, and family allowances, and in the mid-1970s was responsible for setting up the child benefit organisation. In 1979 he was moved to North Fylde as controller – one of the computer 'barons' approached with great trepidation by the officials in London.

By 1985, as the role of Andersen increased, so the attitude of the civil servants altered. Originally, says Bankier, his staff took the view that they were the client and responsible for the system, Andersen the hired hands brought in to advise – and they would treat them as such. Even Caines, the most iconoclastic of civil servants, remembers the same attitude. 'We were very suspicious of consultants and the way they operated,' he says now. 'Out in the field the idea was that consultants sat alongside people who worked in the Department and transferred their skills to them, but the responsibility lay with the person to whom the skills were being transferred. The consultants took no direct responsibility for anything and could, if they'd wanted, have walked away and said, well, we've done our best for you and we've told you what to do, and you don't have the skills or the inclination to do it. And goodbye. But Andersen's didn't ever do that. They felt some responsibility and stuck with it.' Bankier was one of the early officials to warm professionally to the benefits brought in by the consultants, and others would take their example from him.

But Spackman, the greatest advocate of the increased use of consultants, still faced an uphill task all the way. 'It really was very, very difficult,' he recalled later. 'It was hard to sell to the internal staff, because they took it as a personal comment on their own ability. They felt that this was a very public announcement of the fact that they weren't capable of doing it. And of course that wasn't the issue at all: it was that they didn't have the experience and we would have had to spend three years training.'

Very few people, even those as bright as the top echelons of the Civil Service (or, perhaps, particularly those at the top of the Civil Service), understood how difficult it was to bring about change in the Department. 'My own experience is that you cannot change fundamentally large organisations from within,' Spackman insisted. 'It's not just a matter of resources or skills, it is a matter of the individuals in the organisation having their own positions to defend – their own structure and their own position in the hierarchy, their own career prospects. In particular change management within hierarchical structures is extremely difficult. You have to train in new ideas, you have to get acceptance for them, you have to actually manage the process of change. If on the other hand you bring in a powerful outside catalyst, in a way the resentment of the outsider is itself a motivating force because the internal organisation says: "Well, I'm determined to show them we can actually do this, and we can manage the change process." But without that outside influence, that pressure wouldn't be there.'

Yet gradually the most serious opponents, such as Bankier, began to respect the Andersen men, now working beside his own, for all sorts of unexpected reasons. 'They brought in that increased feeling of: We work from half-past eight in the morning till half-past ten at night, if necessary, and that's what we're paid for, which rubbed off onto all the civil servants. You'd find the civil servants doing exactly the same. After a time you couldn't tell the difference when you walked into a room whether it was a civil servant or consultant. The motivation rubbed off,' says Bankier.

There was no question about the commitment of the other senior officials to making the system work. But they still went about it in a way the Andersen men found oddly leisurely. Burgess's six-monthly assessment in December 1986, intended only for the eyes of Levitan at Andersen, contained some deeply felt misgivings. Norman Clarke had asked for a review of the Department's client skills in September, had seen it in October – and had since sat on it. When Burgess raised it with Spackman, the director said he would prepare an action plan based on the report – but nothing had happened. 'I am inclined to find this whole area depressing,' wrote Burgess, suggesting they brought it up at their next dinner with Clarke's new permanent secretary, Chris France, who had just taken over from Otton. 'On my part, though, I am somewhat fed up with raising this over the past three years and still seeing no real action,' he added. 'On the other hand, though, there may be real change in the Department's recognition of what it can and cannot do. John Spackman has certainly made a major impact on them in the use of consultants.'

This report was written at one of the lowest points of the whole of the DHSS's Operational Strategy. Burgess had been pressing Andersen to get in still deeper, go for more and more of the projects which he felt some of the other consultants were not handling as well as he could, commit more people to it. Back in Andersen's head office, some of the other senior partners were having misgivings: maybe they should pull back in what increasingly looked like a disaster area?

Burgess set down his thoughts frankly for his partners to review. Firstly, he said, he was concerned by the attitude of the civil servants. 'I have had discussions with a number of senior civil servants about actions that can be done to bring about early implementation of systems. They are not interested. They are much happier to accept matters as they are rather than to change them to what they need to be to get the job done. There really are no accolades for creating a lot of waves. If a lot of waves have to be created to get early delivery, then it is just not worth it.'

By now Andersen's initial hopes in Spackman had faded slightly. They were irritated at Spackman's support for CSC, which they saw as a poor rival, not just in commercial terms, but also in terms of the DHSS project. Spackman, they believed, wanted to set CSC up as a separate architectural power centre, which annoyed Otway in particular. Otway found himself gritting his teeth at CSC's role in an area he jealously regarded as his own, and it was not until 1988, when CSC finally left the LOP project, that Otway finally gained full control of the architecture. 'Spackman particularly nurtured CSC and their alternative power centre,' says one Andersen man, 'and it really made life difficult.'

There were other objections to Spackman. He had seemed perfect in the very early days when he had been quick to see what the consultants were trying to do. In North Fylde, for instance, Bankier, a tough, no-nonsense computer man of the old school, had a lot of time for Spackman. But Burgess, brusquely stomping about Ray House, longed for someone who would bang heads together, lift the tempo, create the same type of time commitment a private-sector company would. No one, not even Spackman, wanted to put his head that far above the parapet.

Spackman, however, had stuck his neck out to the extent that he had, not without misgivings, allowed the role of the outside consultant to increase. In 1982, when the Operational Strategy was being costed, the budget for consultants by the year 1986 was £500,000. In fact the fees paid to consultants, mostly Andersen, working on computerising the social security system would rise to £12–14 million by 1987. Most of that had grown out of that one contract back in 1982 – a matter about which the civil servants were growing increasingly uneasy. Clarke's Operational Strategy Steering Committee was now solemnly warning Andersen that the fees being paid out were too high, and they would need to restrict work done by them – although there seemed to be no plans to restrict the work done by CSC, working on the technical implementation of LOP. Andersen had made a number of powerful enemies inside the Department, as well as some friends. For instance, Eryl Thomas, the senior civil servant in charge of the overall technical direction, was reckoned to be keen to reduce its participation.

Burgess in turn was applying a little pressure of his own. Andersen had worked at the heart of the Operational Strategy now for three years, and was getting to the point when it must either get in deeper – or phase out altogether. The latter was a most uncomfortable prospect for the senior officials who, whatever they felt about becoming too dependent on the consultants, had long realised they could not implement the strategy without them. Burgess bluntly told Spackman that if Andersen didn't get any of the technical implementation work, then 'in the medium term work on the Operational Strategy cannot be sustained by us. We need to have an appropriate mixture of work if we are to work both properly and effectively.'

For his part, Spackman reckoned he had good reasons for keeping Andersen, however impressive, at arm's length. 'I hoped to get a balance between Andersen's – who came from the accountancy business, down a chain of good financial justification, good project management, that kind of thing – and CSC who have always been an engineering organisation, who came down the engineering discipline. And I thought it was a good mix – indeed they did learn from each other. But it has to be said now they didn't ever work well together, and it was a mistake.'

For their part, the Andersen people disliked being compared to CSC, which they saw as a different sort of business from theirs. They also resented the favouritism Spackman had, in their view, shown to CSC. Nothing that CSC did, they argued, could not be done better by Andersen. It was an uneasy working relationship, which would not long survive the departure of Spackman.

CHAPTER FIVE

A SUCCESS *at* LAST

Norman Clarke's original study group had come to some other fundamental conclusions besides the need to computerise the DHSS – the system itself was absurdly unwieldy and complicated, was not providing help where help was needed, and was unpopular with the public it was trying to serve. Clarke himself, along with everyone else in the Department, was having a rough time as the problems in the local offices became more and more acute. The demand for supplementary benefit had long ago taken it beyond its intended 'safety net' status, and had caused it to mushroom to the point where it was the most expensive and difficult-to-administer benefit of the lot. Difficulties and delays in providing it were leading to disputes between staff and the public all over the country, and there were even incidents of personal violence when angry recipients laid about the DHSS workers. 'Clarke had the worst of all worlds,' says Spackman. 'They even had to put up protective screens – and he had a very discontented public, plus a very disillusioned staff in the benefit offices who wanted to do a better job but couldn't. And he had mounting costs.'

This is no exaggeration. From the beginning, the officials always knew they would face a degree of hostility from the unions to the strategy. It was, after all, predicated – and sold to the Treasury – on the basis that it would pay for itself through staff cuts. The combination of the awful working conditions, growing workload and threatened redundancies was an obvious powder-keg which threatened to go off at any moment.

The keg sputtered often in the early years. In Birmingham, 800 staff walked out of the DHSS benefit offices in September 1982, complaining they could not offer a good enough service to the public. In the Department there was a degree of sympathy for the strikers, who claimed that the social benefit system was close to collapsing under the increasing strain of extra claimants. The unions produced statistics to show that in the eleven months up to the previous summer, people claiming supplementary benefit in Birmingham had increased by 21.5%, while the number of staff to deal with them fell by 2.5%. The Birmingham staff returned four months later after the Department agreed to extra staff and a review of manning levels. But in Oxford there was a similar walk-out lasting fourteen weeks, which only ended when the Civil Service unions reluctantly told the staff they could not find enough support to escalate the strike.

In 1984, relations between the Civil Service unions and the government sank even further as Mrs Thatcher announced a ban on all trade union activity at the government Communications Headquarters (GCHQ), its most vital intelligence-gathering organisation, in Cheltenham. Angry Civil Service union leaders demanded the walk-out of their 500,000 members, but few complied.

In the summer of 1984, the tempo of industrial action in the DHSS abruptly increased when 270 staff at Newcastle went on strike, endangering the payment of retirement and widows' pensions, as well as child benefit. Soon it spread to nearby Washington, County Durham, and suddenly the DHSS was faced with the crisis it had feared from the beginning.

In 1983, the Department's permanent secretary, Ken Stowe, in an effort to break the traditional barony of Newcastle, had appointed a tough, no-nonsense civil servant who had done a good job pushing the Housing Benefits Bill through the Houses of Parliament. Derek Chislett was a 54-year-old official who, as he says, went from doing a 'straight job in Whitehall with about six people working under me, to Newcastle where I had 13,000.' Chislett soon became aware of an attitude that had dogged the Department's efforts to computerise from the beginning: 'They told me when I got there that Newcastle was the biggest computer centre in Western Europe, but I don't think they had really accepted how fast the world of computers was changing.' That is, he adds, only a 'minor criticism of the Newcastle people'. But it was only too visible how the Department over years had concentrated its computer resources on large centralised batch systems at the expense of on-line systems in the local offices, where they were most needed. On the other hand, he also formed the impression that the Newcastle people had been fairly lukewarm about the help they gave to the Reading project and CAMELOT: 'In my personal opinion, Newcastle could have said "Let's get on and have a go at bringing computer facilities to the local offices." But they did not.'

Newcastle, under Chislett, was still to be given a vital, although reduced, role in the strategy. Two of the major projects at the heart of the strategy, pensions and the Departmental Central Index, would be at Newcastle, both of them large and vitally important projects which would need the full support of the Newcastle staff. 'Clearly, there were difficulties,' says Chislett. 'But I think Newcastle played its part, reluctantly at first but it was beginning to change when I got there.' Not everyone would agree, as we shall see later.

Chislett had been there a year when the strike, which was to colour much of his work for the next three years, started. 'I seem to have spent most of my time at Newcastle getting ready for a strike, having a strike, and getting over a strike,' says Chislett.

The strike was not called directly because of the Operational Strategy, yet it was the strategy which undoubtedly dictated the manner in which the Department responded to it. The clerical union at Newcastle was dominated by Militant Tendency, which had been fighting a rearguard action through the 1980s to hold on to its power within the Civil Service unions. In many ways, Newcastle was to be their last battle, an area where, because of the computers, they believed they could exercise the greatest leverage. They had long threatened to pull the plug on the computer systems, particularly the pensions payment system, and now they decided to do it. 'It was their ultimate threat,' says Chislett. 'Even before the strike, it was in our minds that we had to get away from this dependence on Newcastle. We could not be in that sort of position. It was like Thatcher with the miners – a considerable threat was there over one's head, and it influenced the Operational Strategy. When this strike occurred, we had already decided we would not be put in this position again.'

In the event, the *casus belli* was the decision to change the shift working patterns, particular shifts which ran past midnight, or started just before – which meant that workers on those particular shifts got paid for working two days. It was an obvious Spanish practice which had run for years, and which the Department was in the process of changing even before Chislett arrived.

Nonetheless, Chislett tried hard to avoid confrontation, engaging in hours of negotiation. 'I am personally convinced that the people at Newcastle did not want a settlement. They either wanted a complete retreat by management, which they could shout from the rooftops, or they wanted a strike. OK, we were changing the shifts and people were losing money but arrangements could have been made to get over this if one was dealing with sensible people.'

Chislett, reporting to Norman Clarke, was under instructions not to give in. Clarke in turn was under orders from Stowe, and from Fowler. 'We said to the unions, we are not in the game of withdrawing here. The Treasury knows of this, our ministers know of this, for all we know Number 10 knows of this. We've got to find a solution. But we didn't and the strike happened,' says Chislett.

Although there would be other strike threats later, this was to be by far the most serious industrial threat to the Operational Strategy. The Newcastle unions tried to persuade the computer staff at Reading to join them, but much to the relief of the Department and the government, they refused, leaving Newcastle isolated. However, no new benefit books were issued, and payments by post stopped immediately, creating a storm of protest from overseas pensioners.

In previous eras, the Department might have been tempted to roll over, but not this time. It soon found a way of dealing with most of its pensioners: post offices were instructed to pay out on old books, simply stamping the back of coupons already stamped on the front when the original coupon was cashed. At the end of 1984, when pensions had to be uprated by 5.1%, Chislett's staff issued new labels which were stuck onto the front of the old pension books with the uprated amount printed on them. 'I, and one or two others, invented that,' says Chislett proudly, 'and we found some people to write a programme and we actually ran off these covers on the machines and got them out to the post offices. And I think it floored them, because they thought when it got to October, when the pensioners were due to get these increases, the ministers would weaken.'

The strike was only supported by about 400 people out of the 13,000, but its effect dragged on for months. In many senses it was peripheral to the Operational Strategy, yet labour unrest was always in the background, adding to the problems of Clarke and his officials rather than to those of Spackman and Andersen. The Andersen man who saw most of it was Dave Clinton, who moved up to Newcastle, where he would live for two years, to get the pensions project under way. Clinton was the first consultant most of the staff at Newcastle had ever seen, and they viewed him more with suspicion than resentment at first. It was a major culture shock for both sides.

'I used to walk through the picket lines each day, fearing that if they had known I was a consultant as well as a blackleg I would have sustained some physical injury. It was a very intimidating atmosphere,' says Clinton.

Clinton soon encountered the considerable tension between Newcastle and the Operational Strategy Directorate in London which would run for some years. If Chislett had been sent up to break the power of the barony in Newcastle, in London he was now sometimes accused of becoming a baron himself. Clinton found Newcastle an isolated place before the strike, and once it began it became even more so. He was given an office and a secretary which he shared with one of the other key officers, and he began with his carefully prepared work-plan for the project, insisting at the planning sessions that the development of the new pensions system, originally planned as a straightforward off-line replacement for the existing one, should fit into the strategy brief. 'And they were wondering who I was and what right have I to say that we should be doing things this way rather than that way, but nevertheless toeing the line – but resenting it all the time. I was only able to give direction because I worked through the authority of the project manager.'

The Newcastle project essentially was to create an on-line system for retirement awards and payments which could be handled at the local DHSS offices by clerks. It posed major technical as well as operational challenges, in that it meant replacing the big-batch computer systems with major new ones, and plugging them into the local offices to a tight timetable. The Newcastle computers would be able to calculate a person's State earnings-related pension, but under the Operational Strategy a new claim could be entered on a terminal at a local office, and that person's records would be immediately accessible on screen – a major improvement in time and efficiency.

The Operational Strategy could not work without Newcastle coming aboard, and that battle was not an easy one. The Andersen people recall on one occasion Clinton and Burgess being called to a meeting by Spackman, who was clearly furious about the way Newcastle seemed to be dragging its feet. Finally, in the middle of the meeting, Spackman got the project manager, Joe Wailes, on the phone. 'Unless you toe the line on this, and walk in step with us, we'll take the whole IT function away from you,' he threatened. 'We'll shut you down.'

It is by no means clear that Spackman had the power to do it. He and Chislett were the same Civil Service grade. Chislett chaired the steering committees on both the pensions project and on the Departmental Central Index, and would report back to the Operational Strategy Steering Committee headed by Clarke. Technically, the project managers working on the strategy who were based in Newcastle reported to him, although in reality they no longer did. Burgess often went to Newcastle for Chislett's monthly meetings, and took time out to review progress with Clinton, but most of the battles were fought outside. Spackman won that one, and Wailes backed down, but it would still be several years before the Newcastle team, by then much changed, would come to support the strategy with any great enthusiasm.

The strike fizzled out before Christmas 1984 after Mrs Thatcher stood up in Parliament to condemn it. She did so knowing it was running out of steam – and out of strike funds – in any case. It would not, however, be the last time industrial action would threaten the strategy.

The strike had highlighted – and heightened – the level of complaint about the service the social security system was providing. By the mid-1980s, politicians as well as civil servants had discovered that the DHSS was one of the least popular ministries to work for. Yet it was a good training ground for higher things. 'In 1985 John Major was promoted from the Whips' Office to arguably one of the worst jobs in the entire administration,' wrote Norman Fowler in his autobiography *Ministers Decide*. 'As parliamentary secretary for social security he answered letter after letter on everything from pensions to housing benefit. Many of the letters were from MPs and raised very detailed issues from the constituents. Standard replies therefore did not work ... On one weekend, John took home to Huntingdon no less than thirteen red boxes crammed full of letters. He started checking and signing at 9 a.m. on Saturday morning and finally ended on Sunday evening.' For ministers or civil servants alike, it was not a happy department.

By May 1985, the Department's own figures showed that one in four social security claimants was being paid too little, and an even higher proportion faced long delays in receiving payments, following the disputes. The conflicts with the unions had aggravated what was already an alarming deterioration of services to unemployed people, pensioners and other claimants. In some areas, rising unemployment and staff cuts had brought offices to the brink of collapse. In April 1985, a riot broke out in Victoria, one of the busiest benefit offices in London; eight people were arrested during clashes between police and claimants, and the staff walked out, saying they feared for their lives. Earlier, one claimant had stabbed another. It later emerged that such was the pressure on the Victoria office that as many as 300 people had often been made to wait for anything up to seven hours in an area designed to accommodate forty-five. As one sympathetic observer remarked, 'For people living very much on the margin it takes the "security" out of social security if they have to go through this.'

Such incidents were by now becoming common: there were 200 serious assaults on benefit staff between June 1984 and

June 1985. Despite extra security guards, windows were being smashed, furniture broken, and entire buildings attacked. In the summer of 1985, there were further stoppages in South Wales, Essex and central London. Help was urgently needed, but help was not even in sight.

The Department's reaction to all this was to set up yet another working party to review the entire social security system. Beginning in January 1984, it took eighteen months, received 4500 pieces of written evidence, and issued over 40,000 consultation documents; it held nineteen public sessions in which sixty-two organisations and individuals gave oral evidence. In short it was, as Norman Fowler later boasted, 'the most fundamental examination of our social security system since the Second World War.'

It was published in three volumes of a Green Paper in June 1985, starting with the portentous words: 'To be blunt the British social security system has lost its way.' True, it said, the system had helped raise living standards of the poorest and provided a safety net for the sick, the old and the disabled. But on the other hand it now cost £40 billion a year, had grown five times faster than prices since the war, twice as fast as the British economy – and was set to go on rising steeply for the next forty years. It was now twice defence spending and larger than health, social services, education and housing put together. Nor was there any evidence that these extra resources were providing better services – in fact the opposite was true. 'The complexity in benefit rules has meant that social security is difficult to administer and at times impossible for the public to understand.'

By now Norman Fowler and the government had accepted that, even with the strategy, big savings in social security could not be achieved. An earlier Green Paper proposal to scrap the State earnings-related pension scheme had been dropped, and a revised plan substituted whereby the long-term cost of the scheme – to the year 2033 – was to be halved to around £13 billion at constant 1985 prices by changing the formula of payments from 25% of the best twenty years of a working life to 20% of the average income for the whole of a working life.

The purpose of the new Green Paper, called 'Reform of Social Security – Programme for Change', had little to do directly with the Operational Strategy, at least as far as information technology was concerned. But it did have a great deal to do with it indirectly. Essentially, the Department had concluded that even with computers it could not deliver the range of benefits now on offer – and there was no point in doing so in any case. The system must be simplified, redirected, made more efficient, and generally reformed, particularly the two most difficult and time-consuming benefits – supplementary benefit and housing benefit. Supplementary benefit, which caused the local offices so many problems, was to be replaced by income support. A new system of family credit would also be introduced to replace the existing set of benefits for low-paid families. There would also be new systems of control and monitoring, and there would be common rules for different benefits, making them more consistent and coherent – and more easily computerised.

'All these changes will be introduced as the social security computerisation programme moves ahead,' said the Green Paper, 'and the interaction will need careful management. The policy changes will help with computerisation by simplifying structures and reducing the range of tasks.'

The Green Paper contained, at the back of Volume Two, a clear if somewhat over-simplified view of the progress so far on the computerisation of social security. The local office micro-computer project, LOMP, was about to begin, it said, as was TRES (to be completed by October 1987). Some minor benefits, such as mobility allowance, were also being computerised at North Fylde, and that system would be working later that year. A study was under way on the Departmental Central Index, which would be the core of the whole strategy – although little had yet happened on this. There would be on-line computer systems at Newcastle by 1989–90 to replace the old batch systems, bringing pensions into the modern age. And finally there was the Local Office Project – 'much the biggest, most important and significant project within the whole computerisation exercise'.

The Paper provided those in the know with a few hints concerning the problems being encountered with LOP. 'The aim is for implementation to begin in 1988 so as to complete the work in the early 1990s. Computerising the varied and often difficult tasks carried out in over 500 local offices by over 60,000 staff is not an easy job. Both the challenge and the opportunity for the computer industry are enormous and potentially very important for future developments in similar large areas of clerical activity.'

The social security reforms that resulted from the Green Paper were to have a considerable effect on the Operational Strategy. A large amount of the development work that had taken place so far on the main projects now had to be altered and revised. There also seems to have been remarkably little discussion between those writing the Green Paper and those, notably Spackman, in charge of the strategy that would have to implement the changes. 'According to many sources those involved in planning the Operational Strategy were not consulted until the Green Paper was published,' wrote Helen Margetts of the London School of Economics afterwards. Eric Caines later told the Public Accounts Committee (in 1989) that some of the problems experienced in changing the supplementary benefit software to income support software on the micro-computer project (LOMP) were caused by the tight timetable imposed. 'It had to be written in a great hurry to hit the April 1988 start date,' he said. However, in the context of the overall problems the strategy faced, the lack of consultation was merely one more cross to bear and doesn't seem to have set the project back any further than it was already. As far as Andersen was concerned, the most immediate result of this exercise was the replacement of the cumbersome system of family support – child benefit, child dependency additions, guardian's allowance, family income supplement, free school meals, welfare foods, housing and supplementary benefit for the maintenance of families with children, and so on – with a new and simplified family credit system. It was, as Mark Otway quickly saw, the first real chance to show what Andersen was capable of, if only it were given an unfettered run at a project. It would not be as easy as all that, however.

Family credit was from the beginning designed for computer networking – the first new benefit to be so designed. Unlike LOP, which pre-dated the strategy, it was an integral part of the strategy – not an important one, but a relevant one nonetheless. However, because ministers set a time scale of only a year to bring it in, it could not, as envisaged, be properly built – and therefore could not be fitted into the strategy as the strategy was designed to work. Martin Bankier, in charge of the North Fylde operation and with overall responsibility for family credit, confidently offered a computer system which he reckoned could handle it, although not within the strategy. Spackman was pretty blunt. 'Martin, your level of expertise on current computer systems is too low within the Department.' Bankier, who proposed modifying a mini-computer system his people had developed, eventually agreed.

For the first three months of 1986, Keith Burgess and Mark Otway were at their most persuasive, working on Spackman in particular but the other officials too. 'You have to do this properly,' they kept saying. 'You can use all this architecture that we have defined and prove it will work; we can create a proper system which will have a big pay-off, because you can have a couple of hundred civil servants working alongside our best people, and they can be the kernel of your teams to do the really big projects. It's a wonderful opportunity.'

Spackman didn't need much convincing, but some of the others did. 'They were going to lash up a semi-manual system with a little computerised index to run this benefit,' says Otway, 'and we absolutely insisted it must be done as a strategy system.' In the event, for reasons of finance and policy rather than implementation, the introduction of family credit was allowed to slip back a year, and a consultancy contract was issued to assist with building the system. Andersen provided between ten and fifteen staff to work on it. Burgess was determined he would demonstrate to the DHSS once and for all how to bring in a large-scale on-line system that would work from the beginning, and he devoted some of his best people to it.

None of it could have happened, however, without the

support and enthusiasm of some of the key civil servants – and the most important person here was undoubtedly Bankier. 'You speak with Martin, and you think: Yes, nice man,' says one of the Andersen men. 'Actually, in my view Bankier was probably the most sophisticated manager they had. Faced with family credit, he first had to be convinced to do something ambitious, as opposed to the smallest he could do to get away with convincing the politicians that it had been done. But once he had bought in, he was wonderful.'

Bankier took some convincing, but listened carefully to Burgess and Otway as they made their case. Having weighed up the evidence in his own time, Bankier became vitally important for the whole strategy. From the beginning, family credit, unlike so many other parts of the strategy, was to go well. It would be run out of North Fylde, and Spackman had another happy thought when he proposed that Bankier take on Philip Dunn, whose enthusiasm for the strategy was infectious, to run it. Bankier instantly agreed, and Dunn became the project manager for family credit, working under Bankier. Once Dunn was in place, Bankier saw his role as one of building, as one consultant put it, 'an umbrella to keep the world away – and that's what he did. And it was a very sophisticated bit of managing the DHSS structure. What it gave us was resources – he contravened custom and practice to get them for us. Later, when his guys went on strike, he was prepared to back the decision that Andersen would ship in twenty-two people to plug the gap, into a room that Mark Otway would control. That took courage and leadership.'

On the Andersen side, family credit was Mark Otway's baby, as the partner in charge. Much more quickly than anyone expected, the project began to come together.

It needed to be quick, because even with the extra year, the Department, with Andersen's help, was proposing to design, build and install a system for handling it in only two years. 'It was a helluva short time scale,' says Bankier. 'But Spackman said to me, "We've got to grasp our opportunity, Martin, and we've got to bring in the expertise from outside so that our friends in the Treasury and the CCTA can't say 'Do you know what you're doing, Martin? You're trying to do a three-to-four-year project, including delivery, in only two." And we said, "Yes, we know, so we're going to have very tight control indeed on this one." And John Spackman was absolutely right – we'd never have brought it in without Andersen's.'

Unlike other DHSS projects which Andersen and other consultants had worked on, family credit was to be very much a partnership between civil servants and consultants, the two working well alongside each other. 'That worked well,' says Phil Dunn, 'partly I believe because the whole focus was on task and product and schedule and not, as was probably pervasive in our culture, on organisation, status, role, office and authority structure. The great plus about building something in a mixed team is that, particularly if it's done under pressure, people work together from whichever organisation they come from and, indeed, at whatever level they are graded, to contribute their bit to the whole.'

It took only a matter of weeks for any latent resentment towards the Andersen people to disappear as the team settled into two of the most pressured years of the strategy so far. 'Family credit was the watershed in the process of cultural and attitudinal change,' says Dunn. 'It meant that people could see that these consultants, who they previously thought of as élite and different, could muck in and work with the rest of them. They would drive around Blackpool with them at three in the morning looking for a Chinese take-away that was still open to buy two suitcases of chop suey to keep the fifty people on the test team going for the next four hours. That was the kind of formative experience that family credit brought to the Department as a whole.'

As the first visible products of the partnership began to appear, morale soared still higher. 'The kick out of being associated with, and of having contributed significantly to, a success in an unbelievably short time – by Department standards – gave my people such a kick that I think some of them are still on the high many years later,' says Dunn.

The Andersen people were certainly not given any favours. Partnership or not, the civil servants claimed their rights in the old building Dunn was assigned in Warbreck Hill, Blackpool to get the project off the ground. The consultants were last in the queue for office furniture and even for offices. 'At one stage we even made a conscious rule to put them at the end of a string of tables with their back facing the rooms,' says one official. 'It is to their credit that they got on with the job despite that.'

Work began on the system in 1986 and it was delivered in April 1988, right on schedule. And it worked, right from the start. 'It was the first of the Operational Strategy systems,' says Bankier, the man who along with Dunn and another key official, Stephen Hickey, probably deserved much of the credit for it. 'It was a new system which was very dear to the government's heart because it was, if you like, the jewel in the crown of the benefit changes that were being introduced at that time. Therefore it had to go right – and it did go right.'

The smoothness with which the new system was introduced acted as a considerable motivator for the subsequent projects. 'It really lifted our confidence in dealing with things like the much larger income support system and the pensions system,' says Bankier. Yet more than a lifting of confidence was needed for that particular project – both consultants and civil servants now felt it needed a miracle.

CHAPTER SIX

CAINES COMES BACK

As family credit headed towards success, the main part of the strategy, where Andersen was concentrating its efforts and people, was making only slow headway through the fog of bureaucracy and inter-departmental rivalry. An enormous amount of detailed work was going in without much to show for it, which led to frustration and anger among the ministers and observers who had been led to expect early – and visible – results. In large swathes of the Department, notably Newcastle, there was still very little evidence that the civil servants had accepted the direction in which the strategy was driving them. 'We spent nearly three years planning the infrastructure, creating a series of tools, and developing management, methodologies and standards,' says Phil Dunn. 'But what we needed was a revolution in working practices and attitudes – almost a revolution in culture that meant we were focused on task, product and quality rather than on-line organisation which had been the case.'

Even so, by 1986, there was some progress. The value of the management plan, worked out so meticulously in those first six months of 1983, had become apparent. It had laid out not just a list of forward work, but also detailed the tools and the standards needed to carry the development work along – and gradually some of the civil servants, working with the consultants, were getting the hang of it.

Andersen, notably Mark Otway and his team, had refined the plan of course, and added some very sophisticated new pieces to it. Otway had seen clearly from the beginning the need for some kind of common 'workbench' which would govern the standards to which all the various different projects would be built, thus avoiding teams duplicating each other's work – which was an obvious danger – and raising the productivity of the various programmers around the country. He and the team, with a considerable input from the Department's own programmers and the hardware and software suppliers, began devising a complex model for constructing and testing the integration of the systems, which would later prove its worth. They also set about creating some common rules for developing and testing the infrastructure on which the network would depend. The Department would play a large role in this, as would the hardware and software suppliers.

Otway's 'programmers' workbench' was intended to enable the people actually working on the individual projects to design and install systems which they knew would, at the end of the day, all link up. Formally known as the Departmental Integrated Project Support Environment (DIPSE), it was as advanced as anything in its day. Otway and his team finished it in time (just), and released it to the teams working on the different projects. The importance of this was considerable: all the components of the strategy – the data, functions, protocols, operating systems, hardware and communications – had to be defined so that they would fit into Burgess's giant three-dimensional jigsaw.

But by themselves, none of these developments, clever though they were – and there had already been several technical 'firsts' – were going to be enough to turn the vision into reality. By the end of 1986, nearly a decade after the Department began to set out its strategy, performance was falling further and further behind expectations. In an attempt to raise morale in the local offices, Spackman had made a video promising relief in the shape of new technology, but there was still no sign of that relief. And the view around Whitehall that the DHSS's strategy was going to come to grief was waxing rather than waning.

At Andersen's head office in Arundel Street, and amongst senior levels in the US, there was growing concern too. Andersen was driven by the corporate belief that if it was associated with something, then it must be a success. The firm was continually concerned that failing, even with such a complex project, would be damaging to its reputation. Burgess had entered into the contract hoping it would grow, but it was now growing in unexpected and not entirely healthy directions. In his regular six-monthly reviews, Larry Levitan was increasingly sounding warnings which Vandersteen and other senior partners were picking up on. They were impressed with Burgess's work, which they had monitored closely, but they were also aware – as was Burgess – of the dangerous waters they were now sailing in. Andersen had demonstrated to the Department it could get things done – no one doubted that. But because of its very success, it had been asked to participate in more and more of the projects, often where the main work had been given to another consultant, and where its involvement was only just enough to get it the blame if things went wrong. 'We are spread very thin,' wrote Levitan warningly. 'We are participating in large, complex projects where we are only a small portion of the total team.'

Nonetheless, work went on as consultants and civil servants continued to work through the programme laid down in the management plan. There were slippages on almost all projects except for family credit, which increasingly stood out as the perfect project. Dunn's 'revolution in culture', probably marked by the family credit success, was still some way off on other projects, notably pensions in Newcastle. At the end of 1986, NUBS 2 was drifting behind schedule, the LOP programme seemed to the Andersen people to be heading still further downhill, and whatever momentum Spackman had originally brought was beginning to disappear. In December 1986, Burgess summed up the last six months gloomily in his regular report to Levitan: 'Application projects have slowly ground their way forward with, in some, the inevitable slippages. Work has proceeded on the infrastructure, but the usual problems of slow recognition of what is needed, slow mobilisation and lack of sharp and focused management, means that all too often the infrastructure work struggles to keep up, or in some instances falls behind.'

In these six months too, although the consultants and the civil servants were working as 'partners' in Blackpool on the family credit system, back in London the relationship was not going so well. The fact that there were now so many Andersen (over sixty) and other consultants working for the DHSS had raised eyebrows all over Whitehall, and the senior officials were being teased by their colleagues about their 'cosy' relationships with Andersen. 'There was quite a lot of carping from Whitehall and the Treasury that the DHSS had lost management control and Andersen's were manipulating them,' says one Andersen man. 'There was a feeling in the Civil Service that they could have accomplished all this another way, that they didn't need all these consultants. And yet they knew they did need us, and we brought confidence that we could deliver. There was a growing view that as people successively ran into difficulties, we became the long-stop fixer, making sure the pieces were picked up, that problems were addressed and the programme was kept going.'

Perhaps most important of all, there was an increasing view across the whole strategy organisation – shared by Andersen – that the Operational Strategy Directorate under Spackman was not functioning as it should. 'The causes of this are many,' wrote Burgess, 'not least lack of sufficient talent and inadequate management control and drive from key civil servants.' Burgess liked and respected Spackman, but there were others in the organisation who increasingly felt that the director's virtues at the earlier stages were actually liabilities now.

'John had more ideas in a day than most people have in a lifetime,' says one of those who worked closely with him on the strategy. 'Sometimes you need ideas to move forward and other times you need to be able to focus on implementing just a few of them. I think we recognised at the time that John had done a lot to take it as far forward as he had, but that maybe other talents were needed.'

The same thought was occurring to Spackman, who seemed to feel that he wasn't getting very far with the strategy. He had not made himself popular around Whitehall as he had attempted his own change of culture. 'They thought he was difficult to manage, and an unusual civil servant,' says one former official. 'They felt uncomfortable in his presence. On the other hand he had caused them to change and to think about things differently.'

Spackman had done three years at the DHSS when he was approached by a head-hunter early in 1987. Would he be interested in taking on the information systems of the whole of British Telecom, then a newly privatised company? He thought long and hard about it. Did he really want to leave the Operational Strategy at this point?

There were those who would later feel that his leaving at that particular juncture was, as one put it, 'John distancing himself before the whole operation folded', but Spackman is adamant that was not the case. 'It was the most difficult decision I've ever taken in my life, because it was such an important thing to see through. We had a tremendously good relationship with the senior people in computing in government, with Paul Freeman and the Treasury's CCTA, with Steve Matheson of the Inland Revenue and other people involved in the computerisation of government. I have to say I did feel I was letting the side down, but in terms of career development it was such an opportunity at BT.'

He left in March 1987, with the strategy probably at its lowest ebb. Fortunately for the DHSS, it had an ideal replacement waiting in the wings. Eric Caines, rejected in favour of Spackman in 1983, was now finishing his stint at the Home Office where he had overseen the Home Secretary's much-prized Fresh Start project, under which a big prison-building programme was launched aimed at providing twenty-six new establishments, eight to be open by 1989. Caines had been given the target of creating over 25,000 new places in existing or wholly new prisons between 1988 and 1995, on top of 6000 places provided between 1979 and 1988.

The decision to bring him back was largely taken by Norman Clarke and Spackman – not without a degree of opposition. Spackman, who supported the Caines appointment, still had reservations.

'It was an extraordinary decision to take,' he says with a slight air of disapproval of Caines's lack of technical expertise, 'because, when you looked around, those with technical experience in computing are very few, and that was a cause for great concern. I was one of the founders of the British Computer Society, and we got sort of hybrid managers, people who have both computing experience and managerial experience. Now the problem was that none of the technical guys were quite ready in managerial terms to run a thing of this size, and I felt it was better to have a strong manager, albeit a non-technical manager, than a technical guy who was a weak manager. Nobody can criticise Eric Caines for being a weak manager!'

Caines was still smarting from being passed over last time, and did not want the job for other reasons. He was approached personally by Ken Stowe, the new permanent secretary, who invited him to take over the Operational Strategy. Caines was initially appalled. 'I just thought it was a graveyard. People were telling me if you want your career to take a nose-dive you will do that job, because that isn't going to be pulled off. There are too many institutional factors building up against it. It's gone on too long, people have lost interest, the unions aren't going to have it. I was told "Don't touch this with a bargepole."

In the event, he did not have much choice. His secondment to the Home Office was at an end and he had to go back to the DHSS in any case. Stowe would not offer him another job in the Department, so more by default than anything else, Caines agreed to take over from Spackman.

Having given way to *force majeure*, Caines's attitude now changed. 'The warnings I was given in a way made it all the more exciting. I thought, Christ, we might as well have a good go at this. My morale was high, I'd just pushed through the prison thing and I'd learnt a lot about will and communications – or I thought I had. I didn't feel much like a civil servant – I felt like a manager.'

The fact that no one else wanted to do the job either gave Caines some bargaining power. He would do it, he told Stowe, only on certain conditions. 'I'm going to need some allies, and the first thing I'm going to need is a team of like-minded people around me who are going to take on those pressures and forces. I want a small team of four or five people (in the event it was seven). And I can't do it unless I can get rid of some of the ones who are around now – they are clearly demoralised and tired of the whole thing, and they just don't have the spirit or commitment to see it through.'

Within months of arriving Caines had moved fifteen out of the top sixteen people working on the Operational Strategy. His new team was a mixture of Andersen people and civil servants, all of them driven by a much greater enthusiasm to complete the job which, at this time, the early summer of 1987, was getting thoroughly mired down.

For his technical man, he brought in Hugh Ryan from Andersen, an experienced and imaginative computer man who would play a key role; Dave Clinton, who had spent the past two years in Newcastle, was brought back to take a more central role. Burgess of course was the overall strategy adviser and coordinator, with Mark Otway, now working on other projects as well as on the strategy, retaining the vital role he had occupied from the beginning of watching over the entire architecture. Those were the key Andersen men he chose.

From the Civil Service he picked Alan Healey, a tough, ambitious man whom Caines felt was a 'real sharp cookie and a very hard driver', as his operations man. Philip Dunn was still project manager for family credit, and he would become a major figure in the Caines cabinet, somehow always seeming to be involved – at project manager level rather than at the very top – in making things happen.

Finally, he chose a young civil servant who had worked in information technology at the Cabinet Office and the Northern Ireland Office. Andrew Stott – or 'Stottie' – was in his early thirties, and understood the world of computers as well as any of them. He had worked with Caines in the prison service, and before that with Caines's wife Karen in the Efficiency Unit of the National Health Service. 'He had a terrific, very finely honed mind, and a will of iron,' said Caines. 'People like him are gold-dust in the public sector.'

Caines's confidence drained dramatically on his first Monday morning in Spackman's old office. The Operational Strategy, however stutteringly, had moved on a great deal since he had departed for the Home Office, and had now become even more technical, with long arguments revolving around the different systems and the architecture. These discussions were in very fine detail, well beyond the grasp of a non-technical person.

'I hadn't appreciated at the time it was going to be such a technical job, and on that first day I was terrified that I was not going to get to grips with it.'

What he did decide was that he was going to get the best

technical advice possible, and make full use of it. He was going to have to trust other people's judgement, which meant coming to rely heavily on his team. 'Since I had no insight into the technical side, all I could deliver was some clear-sightedness about management objectives, about budgets, about timetables, about the aims of the whole exercise in terms of what it was like for people who were at the office end using the system.' He pauses to reflect. 'And a hell of a lot of will!'

Burgess had been urging the merits of Hugh Ryan on Spackman for some time, and was delighted when Caines decided to make him his technical man. Ryan in many ways was the most unlikely member of the team. A laid-back, laconic American with a Southern drawl, he had helped Otway plan the architecture of the system back in 1983–4, mostly on a flying-visit basis. Ryan spoke slowly and sparingly, but with a dry wit which some of the civil servants found amusing, but which others resented. 'When engaged he is the most brilliant presenter of a technical problem in understandable terms I have ever come across,' says one official. Others, however, could never tune in to his style and attitude, and he remained an enigmatic and slightly controversial figure.

Caines, however, would come to rely on him – and to trust his judgement. 'He talked me through and convinced me that things were feasible in areas which I would never have been able to understand if it hadn't been for him,' says Caines. 'He understood my requirements, which as a manager is to have a basis for exercising judgement about what to do, and that I would not have that basis if I didn't understand. He was absolutely terrific.'

Ryan took on part of the role previously occupied by Mark Otway for two reasons: the first was that Otway was now working on other projects and only available half the time. The second was that Caines and Otway never hit it off in the way Caines and Ryan did. 'Mark would never bend to him,' says one of the consultants, 'and Hugh would. Hugh was prepared to talk about futures, and that was fine. But Hugh made some mistakes too, and Eric was too reliant on him.' Some of the professional computer people, such as Dunn, were less impressed with Ryan than Caines was.

The key relationship which was driving the strategy – Caines and Burgess – was a considerable success, however. Caines had known Burgess slightly before he left, but soon came to lean even more heavily upon the bluff Welshman than even Spackman had. 'I found him incredibly talented, but with this fierce will to succeed, both for himself and for Andersen's, says Caines. They all made up, he adds almost wistfully, 'a formidable team. It was the most effective team I have ever worked with.'

Burgess, in the eyes of some of those closest to the top of the project, filled in some of the quite significant gaps in Caines's abilities. 'Eric had some shaky pieces,' says a former colleague. 'He was not very good at who really made things happen, but because he had Keith beside him, that was never allowed to get out of kilter. And Keith and Otway in particular were always pushing to get key people beside him, but Eric would never have recognised them for what they were unless he was told.' Caines, he adds, was 'very good – I have a lot of time for Eric, but he was not everything.'

Where the Caines/Burgess partnership was at its best was in getting key decisions through the top of the organisation. 'Back in 1983, the Civil Service organisation would kill everything with their bland "have you evaluated all the options" approach,' says an Andersen man. 'You would sit in these meetings and they would trot it out: "Have you evaluated all the options?" And it was their way of killing any progress. Because in that culture, the answer "It doesn't matter because I've found an option that works" is not good enough. They would never accept that we had found a way to go forward; it was always, have we found the best? And of course the search for the best is infinite. There is always another option you haven't thought of – always. And Eric and Keith did an outstanding job of getting that out of the way. But it took three years for that to happen, and the only reason it did was because of our success on family credit. I suspect if we hadn't had that, it could have taken another three years. But Eric and Keith were superb at using that to their advantage.'

Given the problems the Operational Strategy ran into that summer, they needed to be.

CHAPTER SEVEN

CRISIS *at* LOP

Eric Caines had been strategy director for just over a week when he received a letter from Burgess. It began with the formal 'Dear Mr Caines' – although the two were beginning to know each other well – and went on to spell out in graphic detail the seriousness of the situation now facing the strategy's main project, LOP. The letter pulled no punches – and could not be ignored. The target date for implementation of LOP was 'in real jeopardy', said Burgess. 'As you are aware, the political implications, not to mention the costs of delay, would be significant.'

Caines of course knew that only too well – as did Clarke and the other senior officials. Complaints from claimants for income support were still rising, and for the officials the thought of having to confess to another failure over getting on-line information into the local offices was almost intolerable. But Burgess was now warning of exactly that: 'It is our view that the present project staffing, organisation, plans and approach to the work are unlikely to lead to a successful delivery,' he said. 'Major changes are necessary.'

The letter was accompanied by a detailed report which Andersen had prepared, and which was utterly damning of the work so far done on LOP: it had not met its staffing targets, the level of skills at all levels was 'inadequate', there was no one directing work at a day-to-day level, the design work was unclear, no detailed thinking had been done about testing, the technical design was behind where it should have been, but above all the organisation of the management team was not right. 'There is no one who is intellectually on top of the design of this system.'

Burgess had made many of these points to Clarke and to George Bardwell, the man who inherited the faltering project from Ian Marshall, insisting that it should be given a date by which it could show promised action. 'September (1987) was, to my mind, the deadline for this.' Now he said they could not wait until September. 'With the present organisation, approach, staffing and plans – they will not deliver.'

It was a savagely critical assessment, made all the more so by the detail with which Burgess backed up every point. LOP, a direct successor to CAMELOT, had been running before the strategy was ever thought of, and before Andersen appeared on the scene. When Andersen was given the contract for the overall strategy in 1982, CSC got the more mundane design and development contract for LOP. In an effort to get it out of the Reading culture, where it seemed to be eternally bogged down, Spackman had moved it to Lytham St Annes, near Blackpool in the north-west of England, in 1985, and had given it a fresh start with George Bardwell. Yet it had continued to miss many of its target dates, and few in the Department were impressed with the state of its technical development. Even from his distance in Newcastle, Derek Chislett, not concerned directly with LOP, could see how it was going wrong. 'The only area (of the strategy) that really worried me was the local office end where we were extraordinarily slow in producing the detailed documentation on how it was to be implemented,' he says. 'Some of us worried because time was marching on and we did not have a plan for actually getting these things into the offices.'

Yet its success was vital to the strategy – indeed the strategy was to a large extent planned around LOP. If LOP couldn't be delivered, there really was no strategy – just a series of stand-alone projects which might or might not be connected up at some future date. It was also clear to everyone involved that the political row that had followed the collapse of CAMELOT would be as nothing compared to the failure of LOP.

Caines, however, had problems on an even wider front. His arrival back in the Department coincided with the biggest threat yet to the strategy: three of his major projects, including LOP, were being hit by strike action. Ever since the strategy was announced in 1980, the officials had been anticipating – and getting – opposition from the Civil Service unions. The after-effects of the nine-month dispute in Newcastle lasted for months, as did the stoppages in the West Midlands and elsewhere.

The trouble that Caines ran into was a Civil Service union dispute over pay which involved a rolling programme of three-day bouts of industrial action. That was bad enough, but what was particularly damaging was the way the unions had chosen to target key bits of the strategy. This was made clear by Bardwell just three days after Burgess's devastating note.

Bardwell, of course, knew nothing of this and made only passing reference to the problems Andersen had identified. He focused on the industrial action – and how to deal with it. 'A new threat has emerged,' Bardwell told Caines. 'Until six months ago there appeared to be no significant threat to LOP from internal industrial action. The project was not part of a larger installation and, by Civil Service standards, its staff were well paid, reasonably well motivated and, above all, well promoted.' Now, said Bardwell, the union strategy had changed: they were targeting development projects directly, and LOP in particular.

The unions were offering strike pay of 85% of gross pay, and the people working on LOP had voted by 69 to 44 to take action in support of the Civil Service pay claim. They had been on strike for three months. On a subsequent ballot, only five people were in favour of a return to work. The project therefore was at risk. And there was, Bardwell pointed out, an even bigger threat: the introduction of LOP was planned to reduce the DHSS workforce by some 9400 posts. Given the support for the strike action in the development programme, the strike action could spread right across the local offices. Bardwell was not in favour of giving in: if the strikers were allowed to return to work as though nothing had happened, it could invite a repetition of the action and allow the trade unions to dictate the pace at which the project was developed. He felt that LOP must not be allowed to fail or to be delayed to such a point as to be indistinguishable from failure, and set out some ways of dealing with it, ranging from putting the whole project out to the private sector (a 'total turnkey approach') to bringing in more consultants.

Caines by that stage was not at all surprised by Bardwell's assessment of the industrial situation – he was encountering it everywhere. 'All my projects were at a standstill, in perpetuity almost. I mean they were just dead. Nothing, but nothing, was happening.' There seemed to him no point in endless negotiations with the unions which would not solve anything. The mood at the time was to be tough on the unions – Mrs Thatcher had refused to budge on the GCHQ situation, had won the miners' strike, and the unions everywhere in Britain were in retreat, and that encouraged Caines to face it head-on.

'And so, after various councils of war, I decided that if these people understood so little the need to be committed to these projects and to get them into line, then they had a choice: they could come back to work and help us deliver this project or they could stay on strike and go somewhere else,' he says.

It was a fairly belligerent attitude from a top civil servant, even in the heady aftermath of three Thatcher victories. government departments like to feel they are achieving things, but civil servants by their nature do not like ructions. Caines was about to make himself one of the most unpopular people in Whitehall.

By that stage he didn't care. One of his earliest moves had been to map out a programme for the strategy which he was determined, whatever the cost, to stick to. This involved different projects 'going live' or being 'rolled out' on certain dates. The big one, of course, was the local office project, where the roll-out date seemed to be retreating further and further, and Caines determined he must stop that. Having listened to expositions from Burgess, Ryan and others, he set a target date: 27 February 1989, less than eighteen months away. It was a date he would easily remember: it would be his fifty-third birthday. Pensions would follow two months later. 'And what we said to one another was, "We're going to hammer some pegs in the ground here, and come hell or high water, we're not going to move those pegs. We have to have this fundamental discipline, and that's it, that's when it goes live, and we will work back from that date. We will make sure that all that has to be done is concentrated in that period, and we will direct the resource at that particular programme." '

The dates, of course, could not be met unless the industrial action was solved first. During the summer, Caines got his own organisation into shape with a major re-organisation of the Operational Strategy Directorate. He also moved the management of the systems projects in the central offices in Newcastle and North Fylde out of the direct management of the Department and brought them under a new projects manager, Alan Healey, who had worked on the strategy for two years by that stage. He wanted a new project manager for LOP as well, in the hope that this would re-energise it. Burgess argued that, in his view, some of the industrial relations problems were 'a smokescreen' for more serious problems with LOP, but even so the unions had to be tackled. The Caines plan was to concentrate all the available Civil Service skills in the areas they were best at: completing the detailed logical design and programming, although Andersen was finally asked to get involved seriously in the project to help them, after four years on the outside. The physical design and technical development work he would put into the hands of the CSC consultants. Teams from both Andersen and CSC, Caines decided, would work as part of the management hierarchy and would be accountable, like anybody else, to the project manager. This, he explained to Chris France, the permanent secretary, and to Norman Clarke, was a 'drastic move both in relation to the use of consultants *per se* and the manner in which I want to use them, and will be resisted strongly by the trade unions, however it is presented.' But if LOP was to move forward at all, 'that resistance will have to be overcome.' Hiring the extra consultants would be expensive – probably about £10 million, less the savings on the civil servants who would be made redundant or moved – but for once the Treasury was sympathetic. It understood both the importance of LOP and of not giving in to the unions. The money would be forthcoming.

At the Department, the senior officials agreed to go along with it, but they were not ecstatic. There were now eighty-five people working on LOP who were on strike. Caines gave them two days' notice to get back to work or be removed from the project.

Having dropped that bombshell, he called a management

meeting to tell the team he had got approval for his actions from the permanent secretary and the Secretary of State. Even while he was in the meeting he had a phone call. 'You've forgotten to tell the unions about this,' said an angry official. Caines, however, was unrepentant. 'If we'd got into a debate with the unions about this it would have gone on endlessly, and we'd have started making compromises. It needed doing and it needed doing quickly and decisively. There was as much in the message as in the fact of what was being done. There was disloyalty, and lethargy and a lack of interest in what we were doing – a lack of personal commitment.' All of that needed to be changed, or the Operational Strategy was effectively dead.

In July 1987, Caines invited Andersen to complete the functional design of LOP, and in August, under Mark Otway's leadership, it was in. It was all done in such a hurry that there was no time for the niceties of competitive tendering. CSC, whose project this still technically was, now felt it was being edged out. CSC had thrived in the Spackman regime, but under Caines got a much rougher ride. However, CSC proposed a fixed-price development for the work it was doing, and in the case of Andersen, the Department went ahead on the basis that the contract would cost £5 million and save £7 million a month in postponed cost savings. By October, however, they were still squabbling over the details of the CSC and Andersen contracts, by which stage Andersen reckoned its costs would be £11 million. Caines insisted on a warranty on the work they were doing, and finally they arrived at a compromise: Andersen would take on specific tasks on a consultancy basis, working with civil servants as well as the CSC consultants. It was not ideal, and would fall apart in early 1988 when CSC finally lost primacy.

Yet this was to be a turning point in the whole of the Operational Strategy – and in particular in the way in which the consultants worked inside the Department. But as for Caines, he had become the butt of trade union anger all over the public sector. There were caricatures on notice boards depicting him as a Dracula figure with dripping fangs, squeezing large numbers of people in his hands, and the caption: 'Is this the sort of management we've got now in the Civil Service?'

Caines, however, was just hitting his stride. Still unhappy, in early 1988, with the technical work on LOP, he replaced CSC almost entirely, awarding most of the consultancy work to Andersen. The Andersen contribution was now rising ever more steeply to the point where over 200 people were employed in different DSS projects, some in Lytham, in Newcastle, in Reading, in Livingston and, of course, in London. Whereas before a failure of the Operational Strategy through the collapse of LOP or one of the other non-Andersen projects would not have been too damaging for the firm's reputation, that was no longer so. Andersen's name, and probably Burgess's and others' careers, were now, rightly or wrongly, on the line.

That summer, writing his regular six-monthly assessment for Andersen, Larry Levitan worried about the firm's high level of exposure. He had arrived in London in mid-July and, after reviewing the work done, attended the regular dinner Burgess always arranged. Martin Vandersteen, the senior partner on the consultancy side, was also there, while Chris France, Clarke and Caines came along from the Department. Vandersteen had overall responsibility for the quality-assurance programme, but Levitan would take a wider view. The quality-assurance checking at Andersen is an elaborate affair: besides Vandersteen and Levitan, an expert on social security benefit systems, Tom Ross from the Washington office, had also conducted a number of reviews. At a lower level, Burgess continually reviewed the projects he was not directly supervising, while three of the other partners, Mark Otway, Ron Rolland and Hugh Ryan, attempted to cross-check each other's strategy and direction.

Both Levitan and Vandersteen were still concerned that, in the growing panic to get things done, Andersen was spread even more thinly across too many projects. 'Our participation is visible enough that if a project were to run into problems we would be exposed,' said Levitan.

Nonetheless, both he and Vandersteen remained happy enough with the way Burgess was handling it. 'Project risks are clearly understood and continuously monitored,' he wrote. 'We have an excellent relationship with the senior executives of the client and the overall quality of our work is very good.'

With LOP beginning to respond to the injection of dozens of consultants, Caines turned his attention to some of his other problems. Before he had arrived, it had been decided that there should be four major computer centres scattered around Britain, largely to 'map in' to the postal distribution network to meet the first-class post; a secondary objective was to provide protection against further union action. It soon dawned on the new director, however, that this was not as foolproof as some might have thought: he discovered that if the system at Livingston, for instance, was knocked out, the whole top third of the country would not get their benefits because there would, once the system came into effect, be no manual systems to fall back on. The unions, he decided, must not be allowed to staff the Livingston centre.

The site chosen for the Livingston centre was in one half of a new building shared with an unemployment benefit (NUBS) data centre. 'I went up to this building and it was superb,' says Caines. 'And I just couldn't accept that they would let people in who, whenever they felt like it, could bring the whole operation to a halt.'

He explained this directly to the then Secretary of State, John Moore, who had replaced Fowler in June 1987, and Moore instantly supported him. 'This was really critical,' says Moore now, 'one of the most important points in my time at the DSS.' Caines immediately began work on privatising the centre, discussing the possibility of it being run by the General Motors subsidiary Electronic Data Systems, which specialised in operating computer centres. The whole plan had to be prepared in deepest secrecy, with Moore and Caines both exceptionally anxious that there should be no leak even from senior civil servants who would not be sympathetic to the move. The papers were, says Caines, the 'hottest property in Whitehall for a few months before we actually did it.'

Moore became personally involved in this operation, with a series of meetings with EDS through the spring and summer of 1989. He even flew to Houston to see them, going through endless presentations both from EDS and from Andersen over how it could be done. On what was almost his last day in government – he had already decided to resign – he went to Margaret Thatcher to get her support, before he gave Caines the go-ahead.

When the unions heard about it, the reaction was immediate – which was what Caines intended. 'I started getting messages from this lot saying "You try to privatise the other half of this building and you're in trouble. We walk out and there will be no unemployment benefit pay for as long as you want that situation to exist. Just don't try it on." ' The Livingston building happened to be in the constituency of Robin Cook, Moore's opposite number in the Labour shadow cabinet, which gave the situation an added twist.

Caines went up to Livingston again to hold two meetings with the staff, each one with about ninety people.

'I felt, in for a penny in for a pound,' he says. 'And the message I gave them – and the reception was staggering – was, "Look, we're going to privatise this service. I'm telling you today that if you walk out of here now and I have a private team in the other half of this building, you will not come back. I give you that as my firm guarantee. You stay here, and insofar as there are jobs going on the other side – and EDS have decided they want to recruit some civil servants to fill some jobs anyway – I will give you a fair shot at those jobs." The union officials were refused admission to the centre. I had a delegation come to see me and say, "That's the first time anybody has treated us like grown-ups. You put the case to us in all its harsh reality. We want our jobs here, and we would like to have access to jobs in the next building." And EDS were offering very good terms as it happened. So the staff there said, "We'll do a deal with you, we won't cause you any trouble, you just give us access to whatever there is going." And they went away. And the unions nationally were apoplectic. I got vilified left, right and centre in the press.'

But, Caines adds, the 'clincher' at Livingston was that on the day the first people from EDS walked into the building there were forty to fifty people, sitting in a coach at the end of the road, ready to take over the unemployment benefit centre if people walked out. 'They came in from all over the place, and they were just sitting there – and nobody walked out because they knew if they did, they would not come back.'

The computer centre in Livingston eventually came into operation on the day it was scheduled to, and, still run by EDS, is working well, alongside the Unemployment Benefit Computer Centre, still staffed by civil servants. Two of the other computer centres, vital to the successful operation of the strategy, were put out to contracted labour services. The fourth, still run by what are now ITSA staff, is also managing well in the competitive environment.

CHAPTER EIGHT

NEWCASTLE BUYS IN

There were three major components of the Operational Strategy that would make a serious difference to the lives of Britain's social welfare claimants: income support (or supplementary benefit) was obviously one, and because of its complexity and the difficulties it posed to the computer experts, it attracted most attention and effort.

But it was only one of the three, and while work was going on to get it right, consultants and officials alike were equally busy on the other two: a new on-line retirement pension system to replace the old one at Newcastle; and, third, a new system for unemployment benefit, NUBS 2, following some months behind the other two.

The three were all inter-related: 40% of unemployed people also get income support, as do 25% of pensioners. There were other components, of course, but, compared to these three, projects such as family credit and disability benefit were small.

To get the system functioning properly, all three sets of information, constituting a fair portion of the 'whole person', had to be fully and instantly available on a terminal in the local offices – that essentially was what the strategy was about, and what the Local Office Project (LOP) meant.

In timing, Version 0 of pensions was due to go live in the central offices and pilot local offices in October 1988 – the same time as the Departmental Central Index, and six months before the LOP income support system.

The main pensions system, Version 1, which would automate 80% of all pensions work, and which would be able to assess most claims, issue claim packs, provide full on-line information, deal with queries and make payments, was projected to go live on 24 April 1989, two months behind LOP, and be rolled out in the pilot offices over the early summer. It was a project that had started with one consultant (Dave Clinton) and eleven staff in 1984, and would build to a peak of sixty-seven consultants and 160 civil servants (plus another seventy-five from the user community) and, like everything else, would not be without its problems.

Technically, pensions was probably the least difficult of the major projects, although the scale of it was big enough – there were 11 million pensioners living in Britain and another 500,000 overseas. But the big advantage over other projects was that pensions had been computerised for years and the information was available on magnetic disks in Newcastle. When Andersen was appointed in 1982, there was a project already in motion for the updating of the existing computer system, but it was a limited, unimaginative plan that entailed replacing and updating what was there already: an off-line system, in a site a long way from London and the south-east, which would do little to speed the flow of information to the local offices.

The decision to make it on-line was taken early on in the strategy planning, but the team in Newcastle would continue their rearguard action for years. Dave Clinton discovered from the beginning of his work on the pensions project the full scale of resentment in this almost independent barony.

The planners in London could see that officials in Newcastle were far from keen on the proposals to upgrade their own programme, and it was an uphill struggle to force it through. 'I said, no, we've got to change direction because ultimately it's got to be made on-line, it's got to be made accessible to the local offices,' says Clinton. 'It was a tremendous cultural shock to them – they were startled and resented it at the same time.'

The battle with Newcastle had been a feature of the strategy through most of the mid-1980s, and by 1987 was still far from over. The reputation of Chislett, the all-powerful controller, far from being damaged by the strike, was actually enhanced by it, despite the cost to the government of around £150 million. He moved on soon afterwards to the key position of principal finance officer in the DSS, one of the leading Grade Three posts, which he held until his retirement at the end of 1988, to be replaced by Stephen Thorpe-Tracey, who was to be the last of the much-feared 'Newcastle barons'. In Chislett's time, the Newcastle controller was a Grade Three civil servant, answerable only to his Grade Two boss, then Norman Clarke, who was director of social security operations. But in 1989, Partridge downgraded the post and started breaking up Newcastle Central Office into separate projects and units, paving the way for the introduction of the new agencies in April 1991.

All that lay ahead however, and culture change was slow to reach Newcastle. But by the time Clinton returned to London in the spring of 1986, the plans for the new on-line system, designed to be plugged into the local offices when they were ready for it in 1989, were progressing. It would be a much more user-friendly system, geared to greater accuracy with regard to pension claims and assessment processing. Some 99.5% of cases would be handled automatically, saving the government £1.6 billion a year.

That at least was the aim, and when Caines took over in the spring of 1987 he was encouraged to believe it was possible. When the strategy director focused on the pensions project late in 1987, there was a team of eighty-five civil servants working on it in Newcastle, with half a dozen Andersen people supporting them. But progress seemed to be slow, and Andersen began to worry seriously about it slipping behind schedule.

In the autumn of 1987, Burgess sent Al Donald, another bright young consultant, up to Newcastle to take a hard look at the progress being made. Despite his relative youth, Donald was a comparative veteran in the delivery of large-scale systems, having worked in the City for Andersen for five years, installing systems for some of the big insurance companies.

Burgess drafted him into the DHSS team in 1986, and he spent a year on the strategy directorate, working with Alan Healey. Donald's job was to review many of the major projects in the strategy, identifying the problems and weaknesses, and offering solutions on what might be done about them.

Now his mission was to spend six weeks writing a detailed assessment of the situation in Newcastle, which had tended to attract less attention from Spackman, Caines and the people in London because of their concentration on the more pressing problems of income support, family credit and the other systems. Pensions was not expected to be too great a problem, largely because of its long history of computerisation, and because of the manner in which pensions are delivered to the recipient. There was, for instance, little of the immediacy and complexity associated with income support and other means-tested benefits. But Burgess and Caines were growing uneasy about the slowness with which Newcastle was responding, and Donald was to investigate on the ground.

Within a few weeks of getting there, Donald was dismayed by what he found. The problem, he decided, was not so much the expertise of the team working on the pensions project, but their attitude to it. There was no sense of urgency, no commitment and little of the 'can-do' feeling that had now begun to pervade other aspects of the strategy. Donald, encouraged by Burgess, decided to tackle it head-on.

In December 1987, he took the whole team of eighty-five civil servants and fifteen consultants to a hotel in Darlington where he went through his conclusions. A confident, tough Glaswegian, Donald was nothing if not direct. There was a major problem, he told them, and it seemed to him that a large number of them refused even to accept there was a problem. The fact of the matter was, he said, that, with this team working on it, the pensions project was not going to be delivered by its scheduled time. It was clear to him and others that many of the team were simply not 'buying in' to the solutions Andersen was outlining for the project.

To Alan Healey and Eric Caines, Donald was blunter still. There was no point in bringing in a fresh batch of consultants or other skills to supplement the Newcastle team, he said. There would have to be a large-scale clear-out of the pensions team. There was no way he could see of retraining them: 'That would be such a lengthy process that we wouldn't be able to focus on the real thing, which is delivering work.'

There were, as Donald acknowledged, some first-class men working on the team, but they were being held back by the others. Donald recommended keeping what he called the

'A players' and even those 'B players who want to play ball'. But those who either didn't have the skills or weren't interested in signing up for the necessary culture would have to be released and given jobs elsewhere.

'The difficulty,' says Donald, 'was that many of the civil servants who could follow new legislation and policy extremely well had never developed and delivered a major on-line system to tight time scales.' They had delivered big systems using the old architecture, but very seldom with any real-time constraints. For years they had been used to deadlines that slipped, and schedules that were replanned, leaving them relatively free of the type of time pressure which the strategy was now imposing on them.

Donald presented Healey and Caines with a choice: they could either meet the April 1989 deadline for roll-out and make changes – or they could fudge and let the project slip by six months or a year. 'We can have a much easier life in Newcastle if we do,' he said.

Caines was in no mood to let the project slip, but Donald's proposed clear-out of the pensions team presented him with another headache. He himself had set the date for the pensions implementation – 9 April 1989 – and he was determined to stick to it. He therefore had to accept the Andersen assessment that without drastic changes to the pensions team they were not going to make it.

In forcing through the changes, he knew he had a major advantage on his side – the strike at Newcastle had so soured the Whitehall view of the people who worked there that there would not be no huge opposition to the measures Donald proposed. Nonetheless, it took a degree of courage to go to the most senior officials and persuade them to allow him to get rid of half the Civil Service team working on the strategy in Newcastle and replace them with consultants. But he did it – and the Whitehall mandarins agreed readily enough. 'It took a lot of balls on the part of Caines to implement that,' says an Andersen man. 'This was big-time stuff.'

Andersen now brought new people into all parts of the pensions project, taking its team up to fifty people. The consultants complemented each of the major civil servants in key positions with one of their own people, Donald for instance working alongside Dick Martin, who was the project manager.

Here again we have an aspect of consultancy which is not generally understood by those who have not worked in it. Andersen essentially had been brought in to advise on how to put in place a technically advanced on-line computer system. The architecture of that system was obviously vitally important, but the technical side was not everything. In Newcastle, the Civil Service team was perfectly capable of producing – eventually – an on-line system, if it could commit itself wholeheartedly to doing so.

What Donald was now dealing with was a people problem – persuading hard-bitten professional civil servants, who had been working on computers for far longer than he had, to 'sign up' to a new way of working. 'I had to make them sign up to deadlines, sign up to quality, sign up to a change of mindset – and it wasn't easy. In fact it was the biggest challenge I have ever undertaken,' says Donald. It is an area which the Civil Service on its own would have had enormous difficulties getting to grips with.

To lift the morale, Donald had to do what Andersen had been trying to achieve elsewhere – find some quick successes. He started by bringing some of the work forward to demonstrate the kind of live system that was already working elsewhere in the Department. Andersen made up small pieces of design, set a target of, say, two weeks to complete them, and then, with considerable fanfare, demonstrated that it had been done.

The design phase lasted about eight months, and during that time the team held ceremonies every two or three weeks. 'We made a big thing of it,' says Donald. 'We made everything very visible, with lots of graphs on the wall, and we would show who was ahead and who was behind, really personalised it – which teams were doing well, which teams were doing badly.' Donald extended the system right down the line, awarding little prizes for the best programmer of the week, for the most productive team of the week, and denoting which team was 'set for relegation'. The winners got a bottle of champagne when the results were made known each Friday. 'And it worked,' he says now. 'They bought into it – but it took time.'

In fact it took about four months before the environment began to change noticeably. By April 1988, Andersen and the pensions team had what Donald proudly calls 'a production-style project with the right attitude, the right mindsets, where things were being produced regularly.' It had been hard work, but the breakthrough had been made. The civil servants who had warmed to the project were being promoted – and many of them would go on to much higher things – and were beginning to enjoy the new culture (the pensions team at Newcastle today is one of the most efficient 'software shops' in the Department's Information Technology Services Agency, ITSA, which eventually subsumed the old strategy directorate).

The programmes produced in this period were instantly put in place, and worked perfectly. But roll-out was still a year away, and Donald felt that was too distant a target without a visible success he could show to everyone.

That summer he managed to get the system into a few local offices as an experiment, and watched with delight as they settled in well. 'The team worked flat out to get the system in on time and running, which was great, and having got that in, that was the springboard for a much harder piece of work, which was the real system, the big system, coming along in April 1989. Had we not gone for that strategy, we would have been in some trouble in the autumn of 1988 and it would have been very difficult.'

The pressures on Donald and the team in Newcastle were very different to those on the strategy teams elsewhere, particularly in income support, and the Local Office Project. The old pension scheme had developed over many years and functionally was very rich. The computer people at Newcastle had been adding bits to it over the years, and unlike other parts of the system it was in no danger of falling into disrepair. In Newcastle, the team could watch dispassionately as the other teams struggled on income support, which was very much the problem area. Complaints from the public were generally about income support and unemployment benefit – they were much less often about pensions, which functioned fairly well. In many ways, the pensions team was isolated from the rest of the strategy, left to get on with its work once Donald had changed half the team.

The political pressure was on getting an on-line system for income support, rather than pensions, available in the local offices, which was the important deadline in Caines's mind. Nonetheless, Caines and Burgess were determined to hit the pensions deadline, albeit for different reasons than for income support. 'The key thing for us was the political imperative,' says one Andersen man, 'and the importance to Eric Caines and Alan Healey and the Operational Strategy in general that we got the thing up and running on time. We had to demonstrate that income support would go live on time, that pensions would go live on time, because that would be the great precedent for all the other new systems which had been lined up for the future.'

Was there ever a pressing business case for pensions to go live on 24 April? Al Donald pauses to consider. 'No, absolutely not. It could have slipped a week, it could have slipped two weeks, even a month. That was not the issue. The issue was the political importance of demonstrating that these big systems could be delivered on time and actually work.'

There was still a risk, of course, but it was political rather than technical – the system worked rather better than the Andersen consultants expected. 'The risk here was the political exposure of getting it wrong,' says Donald, 'getting wrong payments to a fairly articulate part of the population. Major Sniffling down in Cornwall notices he has twopence less in his pension and writes to *The Times* or the *Guardian* to complain about the new system. These are all big-ticket items and we spent a lot of time worrying about what safety nets we had put in place to make sure that the payments that went out the door were correct.'

Donald was able to try out the system in a model office

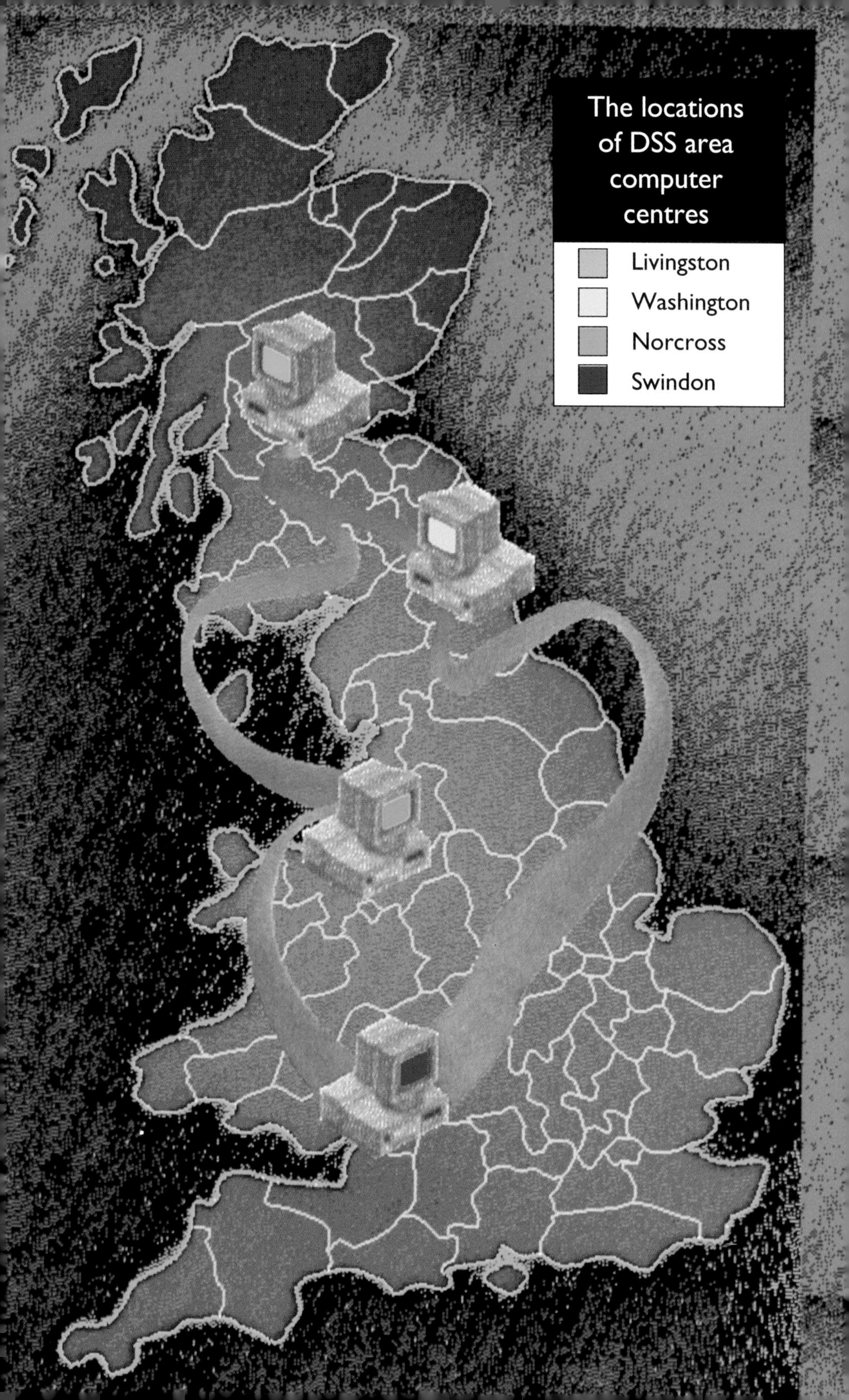
The locations of DSS area computer centres
Livingston
Washington
Norcross
Swindon

Keith Burgess
Managing Partner, AC, UK.

David Clinton
Partner, AC, UK.

Al Donald
Partner, AC, UK.

Mark Otway
Partner, AC, UK.

Ian Watmore
Partner, AC, UK.

Sir Michael Partridge
Permanent Secretary, DSS

Michael Bichard
Chief Executive, Benefits Agency

Philip Dunn
Deputy Chief Executive,
Director of IT Services, ITSA

Kevin Caldwell
Development Director, ITSA

John Kenworhty
Chief Executive, ITSA 1990-92

Eric Caines
Director, Operational Strategy 1987–88

John Spackman
Director, Operational Strategy 1984–87

DSS

Grand total benefit expenditure by broad groups of beneficiaries 1978–9

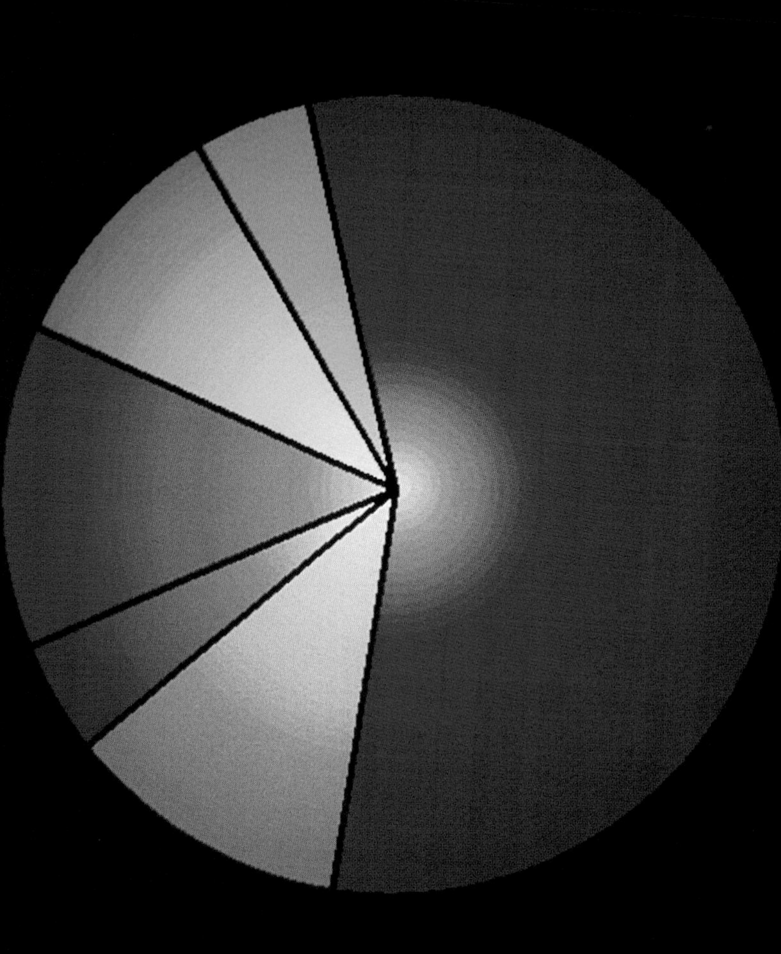

Elderly people	56.3%	8,300 £ million
Family	13.3%	1,960 £ million
Long-term sick and disabled people	11.9%	1,750 £ million
Unemployed	9.0%	1,320 £ million
Widows and others	4.8%	700 £ million
Short-term sick people	4.8%	700 £ million

Grand total benefit expenditure by broad groups of beneficiaries 1992–3

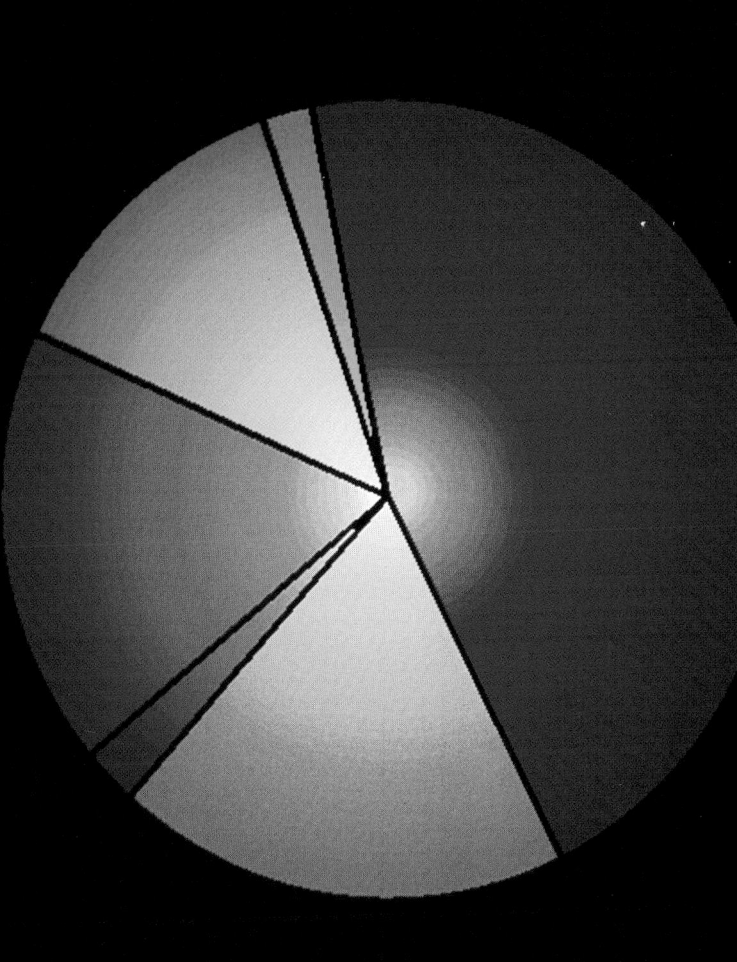

Elderly people	46.5%	34,480 £ million
Long-term sick and disabled people	20%	14,860 £ million
Family	17.4%	12,930 £ million
Unemployed	12.5%	9,290 £ million
Widows and others	1.9%	1,420 £ million
Short-term sick people	1.6%	1,160 £ million

Diagram of the geographical view of the Architecture

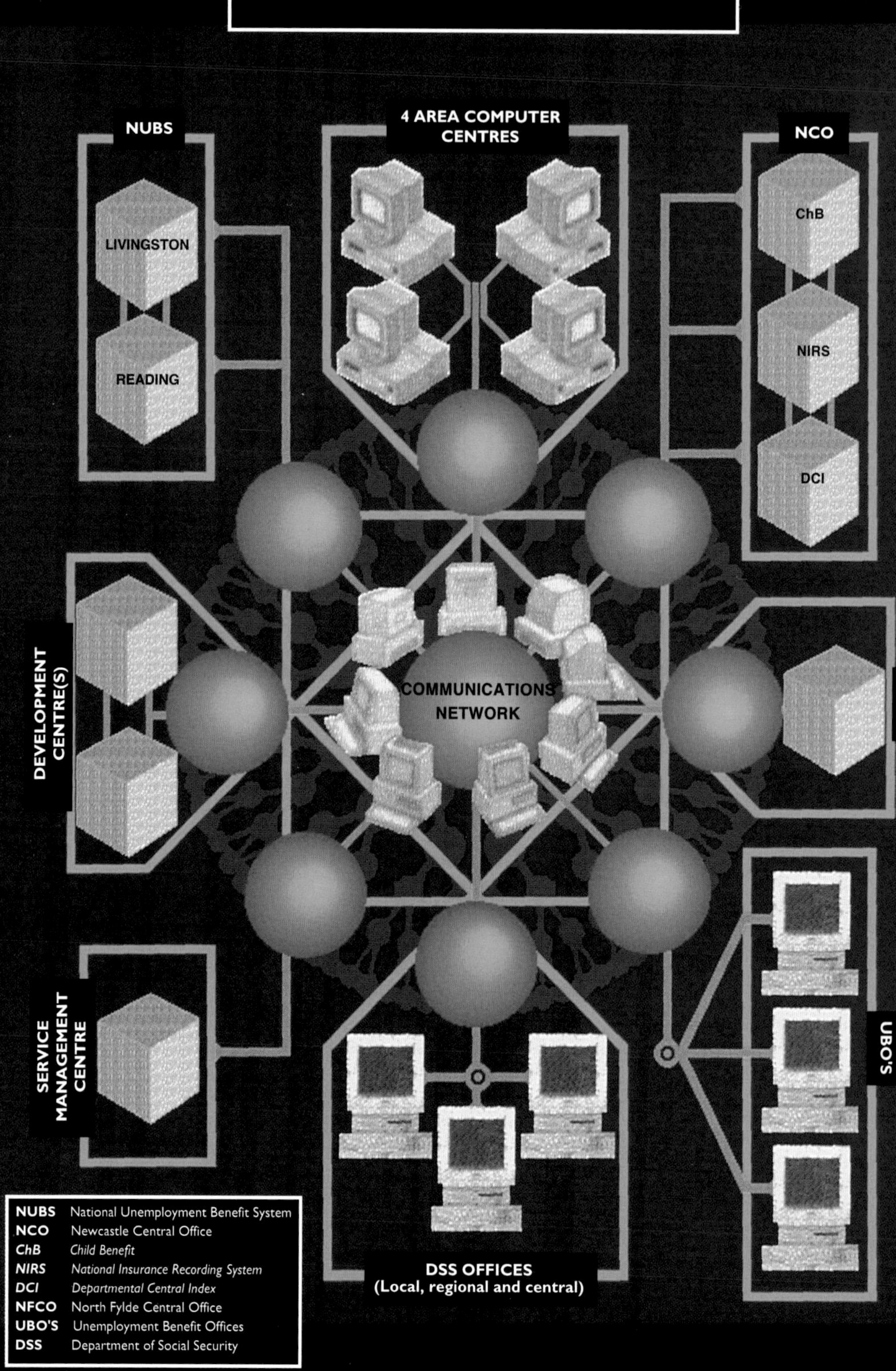

NUBS National Unemployment Benefit System
NCO Newcastle Central Office
ChB *Child Benefit*
NIRS *National Insurance Recording System*
DCI *Departmental Central Index*
NFCO North Fylde Central Office
UBO'S Unemployment Benefit Offices
DSS Department of Social Security

Estimated average numbers receiving benefits at any one time 1992 –1993

Benefit	thousands
RETIREMENT PENSION	9,910
WIDOWS' BENEFITS	340
UNEMPLOYMENT BENEFIT	715
SICKNESS BENEFIT	135
STATUTORY SICK PAY	330
INVALIDITY BENEFIT	1,490
MATERNITY ALLOWANCE	15
STATUTORY MATERNITY PAY	85
NON–CONTRIBUTORY RETIREMENT PENSION	30
WAR PENSION	310
ATTENDANCE ALLOWANCE	765
DISABILITY LIVING ALLOWANCE	935
DISABILITY WORKING ALLOWANCE	5
INVALID CARE ALLOWANCE	195
SEVERE DISABLEMENT ALLOWANCE	320
INDUSTRIAL DISABLEMENT BENEFIT	295
INDUSTRIAL DEATH BENEFIT	25
INCOME SUPPORT	5,320
CHILD BENEFIT	
NUMBERS OF CHILDREN	12,485
NUMBERS OF FAMILIES	6,895
ONE PARENT BENEFIT	895
FAMILY CREDIT	420
HOUSING BENEFIT	
RENT REBATE	3,105
RENT ALLOWANCE	1,210
COMMUNITY CHARGE BENEFIT	6,655

Andersen Consulting, Arundel Street, London

Department of Social Security, Whitehall, London

which Andersen and the Department specially equipped to test the live systems. That also helped iron out some of the bugs, so that when it eventually went into the local offices it was relatively bug-free.

Al Donald had gone up to Newcastle in November 1987 to do his six-week review and ended up staying there, working for most of that time alongside Dick Martin. By April 1989, the system was being rolled out live into the local offices at a rate of six offices a week. By July 1991, the whole of Britain would be converted, and pensions would be served by clerks in local offices with terminals connected to the computers in the four computer centres across the country, not centralised in Newcastle.

Well before pensions, or any of the other systems, had come on stream, the Departmental Central Index (DCI), which was at the heart of the whole operation, was operational. Equipped with large ICL machines, the DCI was sited just outside Newcastle, and when it came on stream at the end of 1988 was one of the largest data bases ever created anywhere in the world. It contained personal, national insurance and benefit information for about 60 million people. It replaced a computerised index system previously operated by the National Insurance Recording System in Newcastle, but unlike that index –when everything was up and running – it would be available to all local, regional and central offices of the DSS. The local offices of the Department of Employment, responsible for paying out unemployment benefit, would also be plugged into it. All the new on-line systems would not only be able to access the information held by the DCI, but would also be able to update it, making it the brain of the 'whole person' concept.

Andersen had been involved, with George McCorkell, in designing the Central Index, and resolving some of the complex technical issues inherent in creating such a large, integrated system. But once that had been completed, the civil servants cracked on with it, and it was live and ready when the Local Office Project was finally completed. By that stage, the civil servants working on the project had become as enthusiastic and as committed as anyone. That was the real breakthrough.

CHAPTER NINE

IMPLEMENTATION *at* RISK

The arrival of Caines coincided with – and also accelerated – a major change in attitude across the Civil Service. After nearly ten years of planning and working parties, and five years of actual work, the mood inside the Department was now seriously shifting – although there were still flashes of the old-style Whitehall. Caines remembers one of the senior officials calling him in and saying: 'We have this problem – could you set up a working party to look into it.' Instead of responding in the way he was clearly expected to, Caines exploded. 'I will not do that,' he replied. 'All this problem-solving – you tell me to do it and I will accept personal responsibility for it. It may well be that I will work with a group of people that you would wish to consider a working party, but it will be mine, and I ought to be accountable to you for that, and there is no other way of doing it. A working party can't be accountable, for Christ's sake.'

The senior official stared at him, amazed – but accepted what he said. 'He didn't like the challenge,' says Caines, 'but it really illustrated for me the way things were changing. We were moving into an era when people have to accept personal responsibility, where it's not just management – it's leadership, it's taking hold of things and owning problems and being committed to solving them in a very personal way, and doing what's necessary to deliver.'

The language, Caines goes on, had started to change at that point. 'That language which surrounds the Civil Service makes it as difficult as possible to do things. Incentives are frowned on, so you have to use other methods. The key to getting things done is not to go around beating people up all day, although I do believe at the end fear and anxiety are good motivators. But that's not the best way – you've got to have people on your side. You've got to get them to do what you want them to do, and you'll do that if you can motivate them, and you can only motivate them if you can offer some incentive.'

The Andersen people, usually considerably better paid than the civil servants they worked alongside every day, had all the motivation they could possibly need. They were driven by an overwhelming urge to get on with the job, define what had to be done, work out a way of doing it and a time by which it had to be finished, and then get on with it. After five years, some of that culture had brushed off on the officials, and certainly from the time Caines took over some of the key civil servants working on the Operational Strategy worked with the same drive and commitment as their private-sector counterparts. From the start, the consultants had brought a certainty that the project was do-able, that even if others didn't believe it, they did. They had then shown clearly how it could be done, and set about actually doing individual projects, small ones at first, but adding up to larger ones. As they planned each project, so they created small teams of trained civil servants who could, and did, go on to the next projects. Spackman, knowing well the full value of consultants, had helped break down the resistance within the Department to their use, proving again and again that employing outside experts was the quickest, and therefore the cheapest, way forward – indeed, often the only way. 'It was John who said your ideas about the scale you use consultants is ridiculous,' says Martin Bankier. 'Any project which is on the boundaries of technology, whether in government or outside industry, has to have the best available expertise, and no organisation in the world has that expertise – it's only available from consultants. You can learn from them, but you can never say at any stage we've learnt it, we can now do without consultants, because they're busy pressing forward. You will say, let's bring in image-processing, or you want to bring in more expert systems; well, they're out there doing that for somebody else at the moment and learning how to do it.'

Yet it was only under Caines that Andersen arrived in the role it had sought all the way through: involvement in the programme from top to bottom. In the early days, Andersen had a role only in planning, although since that involved the design of the architecture, it was important enough; then came family credit, and for the first time it was involved in the actual work-in-progress, working alongside DHSS people. The success of family credit, even before it was launched in April 1988, had greatly enhanced Andersen's standing inside the Department, so by the time Caines arrived on the scene there was wider support for Andersen, particularly when projects looked as if they were going wrong. Burgess, Ryan and Otway could now advise, as they had done all the way through, on the overall strategy, while others, notably Clinton, who was in charge of implementation, would actually work as part of the teams developing the key individual projects. For the first time, there was real momentum behind the strategy as the date for rolling out the various parts of it loomed rapidly.

The whole strategy was now approaching its crunch point. Andersen and the senior civil servants had always been aware that its success – and their own reputations – would, at the end of the day, be measured by one factor only: its implementation. In the first three years, they had concentrated on the technical architecture, on procurement, on changing attitudes and culture and so on. But from 1986 onward, when the design problems had mostly been resolved and development was under way, the attention had begun to turn towards the problems of installing the system and getting them to work. The whole point of the strategy was to improve service to the recipients, or 'customers', as they were now known, and to raise the level of job satisfaction among the thousands of disgruntled DHSS employees. And in these areas, the proof of the pudding would be in the eating: the system would either work or it would not, and at the end of the day nothing else would count.

Andersen had been worrying about this phase from the beginning, but in 1981 it had seemed a long way off, and there were other priorities. In April 1986, when Dave Clinton returned from Newcastle, he joined John Moyes, a Grade Five civil servant, in the Regional Directorate, then essentially the headquarters of the entire regional organisation, to begin serious planning of implementation. By October 1986, Clinton and Moyes had produced what they called their Blue Book, which was a review of the implementation arrangements for all the strategy systems. It came to a number of key conclusions:

first of all, it found that although most of the work on the strategy had been broken down into work packages that suited the needs of the systems developers, that work breakdown was not necessarily the right one for implementation in the local offices. For instance, there were separate projects running on the Central Index, on retirement pensions, on income support (or supplementary benefit, as it still was), and the order in which they were ready for roll-out was not necessarily the ideal order for their installation in the local offices. 'If I was looking at it from the viewpoint of a local office manager responsible for all those areas,' says Clinton, 'I wouldn't want them coming at me in a haphazard way.'

He and Moyes worked out a system and timetable which suggested that projects should go live in a different order from their development. They recommended that the Central Index and an early version of pensions should go live first, then the LOP income support project, followed by pensions proper – and that sequence should be followed by most offices. They also tackled the huge problem of how to prepare and train the staff in the local offices for their arrival.

The Blue Book set out the roll-out strategy, which was going to be a major programme of business change – Clinton's speciality. 'How could we get around 500 offices, 50,000 people? How long was this actually going to take? How should we do it – sequentially, or serially? Should we have some sort of staggered approach? And so on.'

Eventually it was the staggered approach which was adopted, which entailed a pilot period in the north-west region and in Scotland, and then full roll-out in each of the five other regions, ending in Wales and the south-west.

The implementation team also looked at another key aspect which everyone had long known must be tackled: the offices themselves. In some areas of central London, the offices were in desperately poor shape, with staff operating in such overcrowded conditions that sliding doors had to be installed because there was no room for doors that opened normally. The fabric of many offices had been badly neglected over the years, and there was no way they could accommodate the new systems without considerable rebuilding work. The difficulties with the micro-computer project several years earlier had given the planners a foretaste of what might happen with a much more complex system. Now they had to think about every office in the country, all of which would have to be converted to accept modern technology.

Clinton noted that the most efficient way of training 50,000 people was to shut each office for a month, train everyone at once, and then re-open the office. Could that be done? 'That became the key question,' Clinton recalls. 'What level of service degradation was acceptable as we rolled out the system?' Clearly, this was a politically sensitive area, and a decision to be taken at the highest levels of the Department. Could they risk the inconvenience of a complete closure of each office, with all the disruption that would entail for short-term benefit recipients? In the end, it was decided that they could not. They must try to maintain the same level of service while training people. That decision in turn determined how the systems would be phased into the local offices.

At his end of the project, Clinton was now identifying a scale of problems entirely separate from the ones being met at Lytham, Reading or Newcastle. Principal among these was the conversion of the mass of clerical papers held in the local offices, mostly relating to supplementary benefit, or income support. There were 5 million files which would have to be converted to the new system, and many of these, they knew, were inaccurate or out of date. 'There was the problem of what were we going to do when we realised we had found errors in these case papers,' says Clinton, 'with the subsequent impact of overpayment, or underpayment, and so on.'

It was an enormous clerical exercise, and part of the Moyes/Clinton strategy was a plan to create a model network of activities for local offices so that they had a template of a local office installation which simulated everything from briefing the local office manager, developing his plans, preparing for case conversion, for training, and everything else. It also included a plan for modelling all the communications and education awareness events which had to be planned for, the scheduling of each individual within an office for training, the actual delivery of equipment, and support after roll-out.

The Blue Book and the subsequent planning sessions were immensely detailed, but absolutely core to the progress of the strategy. 'Increased service efficiency and job satisfaction weren't going to happen by magic,' says Clinton. 'They would have to be managed out. You actually had to change not only the technology but also the way in which people worked – their working practices – and also the people themselves in terms of their knowledge and the skills they needed to acquire, and in terms of building their motivation and commitment. We needed to provide the right leadership, change the management style to encourage those new disciplines and virtues.'

From all of that derived an interim testing system they called the 'early production environment', which would be in place in October 1988, in time for the DCI and some of the pensions to go live, and later, from the autumn of 1989, the more permanent 'full production environment' system. From this too came a plan to build a model office which would replicate all the programmes, communications and workload on an ordinary office.

Early in the process, Andersen arranged for a visit to the United States to see a model office, with all the technology the social security system would be using, actually working. Ian Stewart, in charge of putting the strategy into Scotland, went, along with some of the other regional implementation managers, but they came back unimpressed. They had seen a screen which even after three or four hours' study Stewart says he did not understand. But the principle of mocking up an office, which could test the project before it was put into practice, seemed to everyone a good idea.

To get the model office up and running, Burgess had brought in another Andersen man, David Finn, early in 1987. Finn was given a tough brief by Burgess, who explained to him the unhappy history of LOP. 'We have to make sure that what we are doing now is not going to turn into another CAMELOT,' he told him. Burgess's fear – indeed, the fear of everyone involved – was that the technology being developed for income support would work in the laboratory but would not be up to the pressures it would be subjected to in the local offices. 'The problem is that if you put a system into an office, it must work from day one,' says Finn. 'You can't have it not working, so the training, the system itself, the technical architecture, the job design and the instructors all have to come together.' Finn, in conjunction with two DHSS men – Roger Blackwell and Steve Carpenter – set about building a prototype environment which would mock up an office, and, in Finn's words, 'take these various pieces – because they arrived in pieces – and put them together.'

He spent some weeks driving around north-west England looking for a suitable site for his laboratory. Ideally, he wanted a corner of a working office he could cordon off, but he couldn't find one – the offices were never big enough or were in the wrong place or had some other problem. He ended up in Preston in a government building, where he took two floors. On one, he created an administrative centre where the tests could be planned, and the other would be his actual model office. He recruited social security staff from surrounding offices to man it. Five months after finding the office it was kitted out and ready for occupation.

This was to be a 'user' system, sponsored and adopted by the operational people who would actually operate it, rather than by the people at Lytham who designed the system. Preston was about half an hour's drive from the operation in Lytham, far enough to be independent, yet close enough to link into its systems as soon as they were running. Finn oversaw the cabling of the office to Lytham, making it the first remote link to the new system which would eventually be connected to every office in Britain.

'We mocked up the technical line it would run across, and the end-to-end architecture, which worked out how the mainframes would be linked to the terminal and across what network lines, and we began testing that – and it worked.' The model office also got the first of the thousands of BT terminals which would eventually be installed in all offices. Finn pushed the income support system at Lytham, insisting that he was given pieces to test even though they were not working perfectly yet. 'We don't care if it doesn't work,' he kept arguing. 'That is the whole point of a model office – we can get it from the point where it is now, to the point where it really does work, and then it is ready to go out.'

He worked out what the cabling would look like in an average office, and how the terminals would 'talk to' the controller, which in turn talked to the network. 'Let's build this and get some real people in here,' he kept urging the others. 'Because when you get real people on the end of it they think of completely different things to what we expect. People use systems in ways that the designers never intended, and they don't use them passively.'

In Finn's model office, the terminals were designed to handle both pensions queries (where the problems were already largely solved by Al Donald's team in Newcastle) and income support, where the big problems still lay. They were also designed to have access to the Departmental Central Index, and began processing real information, using the details of the workload in a genuine office in Blackburn, running them a day behind.

What did they learn from the model office? 'An awful lot,' says Finn. 'We had a series of things specifically directed at the implementation side. For instance, there were no computer records for income support, and every office was going to have six months to get the case load on, and for a large office that might be as many as 20,000 files. We did a lot of work on what was the best way of tackling that: do you tackle them up-front, do you wait until a little bit of post comes in and tackle them at the point where you go and get the case file – and there were legions of small things to think about.'

From the model office came the recommendations for the furniture the local offices would need when they came to computerise. The Department invited dozens of different suppliers to tender for the order for some 20,000 desks, and then put a short-list on trial to find the best. 'The model office was turned into something like the Ideal Home Exhibition for a week,' says Finn.

Implementation was always taken very seriously in the Department, planned and debated at the highest levels, but still posing a raft of unsolved problems. It was deemed to be too important even to be left to the Operational Strategy Steering Committee, and was run directly through the Department's management board, chaired personally by the permanent secretary. After Clinton and Moyes finished their report in October 1986, implementation was run by the Department as a line responsibility rather than a project responsibility, which meant the control came from the permanent secretary down through the director of the regional organisation, through the regional controllers to the seven regional implementation managers, each of which had his own team to help local managers through the process. There was of course a strong central team directing and steering it from the centre – which is where Clinton was placed, first with John Moyes and later with Owen Thorpe as his Civil Service counterparts.

The programme of implementation also had to be costed. The Department had always been aware that the strategy would provide a wonderful, once-in-a-generation opportunity to upgrade the working conditions and environment of everyone working in the local offices. But it was also aware that it was going to cost money. The on-line terminal systems required new desks, lighting and carpets, as well as underfloor cabling and so forth. In many cases, the strategy would require complete new offices to replace old ones ('old' did not necessarily mean Victorian or Edwardian – often offices built in the 1960s were just as unsuitable as something built 100 years before). The sensible office managers used the opportunity to give their premises a coat of paint, with the result that by the time that roll-out was completed, the average local office bore little resemblance to the dingy building of the mid-1980s. The total cost of furnishings, cablings and improvements to the buildings was around £150 million. No one seriously begrudged this element of cost, not even the Treasury. Britain's social security system was limping into the modern age.

As the date for roll-out approached, the Andersen consultants were increasingly preoccupied with ensuring that all the components of the strategy would work together. The production environment models were elaborate programmes for testing every element of it, but no one could be sure that one would work until it was actually tried in the local offices under normal working conditions. No one was seriously worried about the ability of the systems to process specific benefits – each of the individual projects had been tested and retested to the point of exhaustion. But would the applications work properly with each other? Could they really deliver, on a single terminal, all the information required to deal with a claimant on the 'whole person' basis? How would the system stand up to the environment in the offices, in the hands of trained – but still semi-skilled – clerks? As roll-out gathered pace, were there enough technicians to support them and keep them operable? What unforeseen demands would be asked of them?

They also had to begin looking beyond the actual roll-out to the management of the system once it had gone live. Andersen and the Civil Service teams began planning a service management centre, which would be sited at Lytham and would be responsible for managing the whole network when it was operational. Most of the concentration up to that point had been focused on developing the individual projects on schedule and testing them to ensure that they worked, and there had been little energy to spare for what came afterwards. 'Everything was planned up to the completion of the different projects,' says Ian Watmore, the Andersen man who would be responsible for setting up what was called the Service Management Group, or SMG. 'But thereafter it was a bit of a void.' Called in by Caines, Watmore and his new team first wrote a plan for managing the systems after roll-out, and began work on another for ensuring that they would run as efficiently as possible.

Watmore worked with George McCorkell, whom Caines appointed project manager for the SMG, and with Andrew Stott, who had overall responsibility for larger and larger slices of the strategy under Caines. Stott was clearly destined for senior positions in the Civil Service, his job now a stepping stone that would give him some line management experience to back up the policy work he had already done. 'He had never actually done any systems work before,' says an Andersen man admiringly, 'but he read every book that there was on the subject. He could cite you chapter and verse about some of the deeply technical things going on in open systems standards around the world.'

McCorkell had joined the Ministry of Defence in 1967, had worked in Newcastle on computer procurement, did a spell with the CCTA in the Treasury, and, on the strategy, had run the DCI project, the LOP technical design, and in late 1987 had replaced Dunn as project manager on family credit. 'He brought the coolness under fire to make the right, sometimes tough, decisions required for running production systems,' says a colleague.

The SMG was built from scratch, an entirely new group within the strategy directorate. Its first task was to put into place the first stage of the strategy-testing environment, a unique programme of testing originally worked out by Burgess and Hugh Ryan and implemented by Otway and his team. They built a small-scale replica of the full production environment: applications, mainframes, networks and terminals, delivering production services (not based on real people at this stage) to Finn's model office. It would provide some invaluable lessons when it came to actual roll-out.

But the main part of Watmore's project was to establish a service management centre at Lytham which would end up being one of the most technologically advanced projects of the whole Operational Strategy. They planned it to be as automated as anything in any industry in the country, if not the world: technicians and staff at a single central office in Lytham would be able to manage the whole system across the country by remote control. Only as a last resort would engineers and technicians have to go out into the country to deal with a problem – everything else would be handled by computers, which from Lytham would tell 25,000 terminals all over Britain what to do. That was to be another technical 'first' for the strategy, one of a number, and a considerable one. From this one room in Lytham St Annes, eighty ICL mainframe processors would be run, linking in to one huge network beyond. 'That still amazes even me, and I was part of it,' says Otway now with a degree of wonderment.

The vision for the SMG centre at Lytham, however, was not

Otway's, but that of Hugh Ryan, who sat down for two weeks early in 1989 with an Andersen manager and wrote out a design for the system needed to support a group, consisting of some 2000 people, which would deliver a service to 25,000 terminals. 'He did an absolutely seminal piece of work on that, which enabled it to happen,' says Otway. 'And it was more of a technical first than anything in the whole system.'

The SMG, as they designed it (and as it now works), would have a help desk of 250 people (now reduced to 120 by use of more advanced technology), each one handling an average of ten calls a day, so that it would be capable of dealing with 2500 problems a day – each problem logged as it occurred and tracked through to resolution, all from the same centre.

The SMG would be supported by Andersen and other non-civil servants from beginning to end. Obviously, there were a large number of increasingly confident civil servants involved, but the vision, the design, the development and even some of the provision of day-to-day technical and management support, once it was up and running, were provided by outsiders. Without the consultants, the difficulties in developing it would have been considerably greater – the production systems controls for pensions, income support, the DCI and so forth were going to be handled from a single desk, and within the Department the different project managers would have needed a great deal of persuasion to co-operate.

But even while Watmore and the growing team of Andersen consultants at Lytham – at the peak there were forty – plus the even more rapidly growing number of civil servants (the numbers involved went from zero to over 2000 in three years) were working on service delivery and management, the Local Office Project was approaching its roll-out date. This, everyone knew, was where the real problems lay – and where no one was yet sure they could resolve them on time.

CHAPTER TEN

ROLL-OUT

Ian Stewart, a civil servant who would play an important role in implementing the Local Office Project, remembers well the moment Eric Caines took the responsibility for LOP out of the hands of the old Civil Service team and gave it to the new regime, including Andersen. A joint team was established under the direction of Philip Dunn and Mark Otway, with the technical design led by another Andersen man, Mark Goodyear. LOP also owed a lot of its final success to a bright young DSS manager – Kevin Caldwell, now Director of the Development Directorate at Lytham. 'It was obvious to all of us that the project was running behind schedule and that the civil servants were finding it very difficult to produce the code and performance that were necessary to get the strategy in on time,' says Stewart.

LOP had defied the technicians long before the strategy was ever conceived, had caused major headaches to Clarke, Spackman and Caines, and was not going to surrender to the new world of technology without a final battle. By the autumn of 1988, pensions was well up to schedule, the Central Index was up and running, work was beginning on a new unemployment benefit scheme (NUBS 2) which would come along behind the others, Watmore's planning for service delivery and management was well advanced, yet a feeling of high risk still pervaded the programme, most of it centring on LOP. 'There was a risk on the technical side – could we do it on time and could we do it within the business case?' says Stewart. 'There was the risk of the trade unions – could we get it past them and actually get down and show staff how it worked? And the third risk was on the operational side, which was my side – could we actually deliver the users, trained, with an understanding of what it could do and how well it could work, given the difficulties we were anticipating on the technical side?'

Stewart, like Caines, is an unusual civil servant, one of the more charismatic men – civil servant or consultant – involved in the Operational Strategy. He still has the shape and build of the professional footballer he once was. He is a natural leader, a man who would drive his Civil Service colleagues with the same energy and enthusiasm as he would Montrose Football Club, where he played until he was thirty. Later, as he moved up the Civil Service echelons, he still found the time to manage the team.

Under the strategy for rolling out the Local Office Project, as worked out by Dave Clinton and John Moyes, it would go live first in two pilot areas with twenty-three offices in Scotland, which was Stewart's patch, and in north-west England, which was the province of Derek Dunthorne. Once the bugs had been ironed out, roll-out would then move on to the other five regions, but the system had to be tested thoroughly in actual operation first. Why these two regions? London was initially the first choice, basically because of the huge pressures there, and it was equally obvious the system should be tested around Lytham, where the LOP programmes were being developed. London, however, posed more problems than it solved: staff were at their most demoralised there, and management was not as good as it should have been. Stewart's native Scotland was a different matter: it was reasonably settled and had a good management ethos and people who actually wanted the strategy to succeed. True, the trade unions were strong there, but Stewart reckoned that was no serious drawback – 'I was confident that they were fairly pragmatic and that they could be convinced of the benefits, as opposed to convincing themselves that it was a management device to get something in quickly that didn't provide any lasting benefits.'

On the way home in a taxi after watching a Scottish International at Hampden Park, he suggested to Dave Clinton that London be dropped and replaced with Scotland as one of the pilot areas. Neither of them had the power to implement that decision, but they agreed that they would both set out separately to convince the Department that this was the best way to proceed.

By the autumn and winter of 1988, Stewart needed all his

energies and driving abilities. Clinton, analysing his own blueprint for roll-out and adding up the business benefits that would accrue from running the system, came up with a radical new suggestion which would make the programme even tighter. Originally, he had calculated that full roll-out would take 3.75 years, which was three months less than the Inland Revenue had taken to computerise its PAYE system. Now he reckoned it could be done in a much shorter period – assuming it began on time. In October 1988, he recommended to Caines and Burgess that if they did it region by region in parallel, there was no reason why roll-out should take longer than 2.5 years. The efficiency savings would be considerable – by bringing it forward in that way they could save £28 million. Caines, impressed by Clinton's logic, agreed to the shorter timetable. Scotland, under Stewart, now became the focus for bringing the LOP income support system live first.

Even with the sense of urgency which Caines had fostered, it was still an uphill task to get the necessary momentum going. The users – the people actually delivering the services in the local offices – had also become more and more disenchanted as promises made to them never seemed to be kept. Philippa Reid, one of the Andersen team brought in by Burgess in the autumn of 1983 to work on the project, recalls: 'The difficulty was that communication really wasn't taking place through the five or six years of development to the point where users were up to speed on what was really happening on the technical side. Now the technical people had signed up to this overall vision but in the real world you decide that certain things aren't worth the investment – you could do them but frankly it's not worth it – so you cut the scope somewhat, you decide that some things are just too complicated. Then you start running out of time and you say: well, am I going to extend the time scale or do a bit less? And all of these kinds of decisions were being made, with user involvement, but not with the wider user-community being kept informed.'

There had been an original 'roadshow' with Spackman's video, designed to sell users on the idea of the strategy, and that had raised expectations that were not being met. In the rush to get the system together and meet the dates hammered down by Caines, corners were being cut, bits left off the system which had originally been allowed for. 'We missed a trick by not having a second roadshow,' says Philippa Reid, 'which said, "The Brave New World we promised you looks like this now and this is how it is going to operate." Some of that wasn't managed well, but I don't think people had time to think about it. The technicians were too busy, and the users themselves were desperately writing procedures, making sure that the implementation plans were in place, doing the physical things rather than the emotional things – so the emotional things, quite frankly, were not tackled.'

In fact there was another roadshow, not as ambitious as Spackman's, but at least an attempt to educate the people most immediately affected on what the strategy now meant. In Scotland, Stewart, who also had responsibility for the overall education programme for the strategy, devised his own roadshow for the pilot scheme. He prepared a PC-based presentation with a 'storyboard', a modern computerised method of presentation, and showed it to groups of fifteen staff in each of the nine pilot offices in Scotland, going back two or three times to emphasise the various points.

After that he had to begin organising the offices physically to receive the equipment being developed at Lytham. 'Some of the offices were in a dreadful state,' says Stewart. Fortunately, his responsibilities in Scotland also included all the Department's accommodation, which gave him an advantage over other regions. Where the responsibilities for accommodation were separate from responsibility for the strategy, the problems were considerable, but nowhere was it easy. Local managers all over Britain had to negotiate changes to their accommodation with the Property Services Agency, the notoriously slow-moving government department responsible for offices throughout the Civil Service. Planning some of the offices in some cases would take several years, particularly where it involved moves into new premises, which was sometimes the case. Premises had to be surveyed and designed, office managers had to replan the internal office layout, making provision for the computer terminals, printers and so forth, then they had to negotiate with the contractors, and get the buildings completed on time.

In Scotland, this aspect went better than in other regions. The Scottish controller, Bob Walton, had foreseen the problems early and agreed from the start that Stewart should be given responsibility for both accommodation and for implementation of the strategy. 'So we actually started two years before we even needed the accommodation, because we were looking something like twelve years ahead and bringing in these massive social security reforms and it made sense to plan long-term,' says Stewart.

From early in 1987 onward, any new office built in Scotland had been designed specifically to accommodate computers, given raised floors and the lighting that would be needed, even to the point of being given special cabling ducts, and as roll-out approached, Walton and his staff were pleased with their foresight. 'This was a very important decision at the time,' says Stewart. 'We actually took all our cables in Scotland through metal-based trunking, which was fully earthed and gave us capacity for expansion. So when it came to implementation, we didn't have the problems they did elsewhere. Screens didn't flicker or fall over.'

These were sensible, simple decisions, partly the result of lessons learned from the micro-computer project several years before. Stewart dashed around the country organising the trunking, setting up special areas to take the local office computers, and creating a brand-new training centre in Glasgow which became one of the showpieces of the whole strategy.

The operation at Lytham was supposed to devise a special computer-based training system for clerks to work on, but like so many operations of its kind, it ran into problems. Stewart took it over and had his own people in Scotland iron out the bugs. His team actually developed the software for the training, which was very new at that stage and was to work well. 'So we now had a direct interest in the training, accommodation and the implementation of the strategy, and the three things were very important to us. And we were able to move from education to putting the accommodation right, to putting in the cabling, to putting the boxes on the desks and to training the people to use them.'

As the months wore on, Scotland, even more than the north-west, became the focus for the success or failure of the implementation of the income support system. Dunthorne was less flamboyant than Stewart, at times giving the impression that he lacked the drive and enthusiasm of his Scottish counterpart, but he was nonetheless respected by those who worked with him. Where Stewart emphasised the positive, Dunthorne pointed out the negative, identifying the problems rather than looking for the solutions as Stewart did. The two complemented each other well.

'It was undoubtedly useful having the competitive rivalry between the two regions,' says an Andersen man. 'One of them would never give up if they thought the other was going to proceed. Until they actually went live and began paying benefit, there was always the possibility of them saying, "No, I'm not going until we get it right", and they could have found some technology-based reason for it, and they would have sought perfection before we started. But because we had two, the Scottish ones weren't going to pull the plug if the ones down in Bolton were going to get on with it, and vice versa. That gave us, from the technology point of view, a substantial competitive leverage to apply in getting people to take sensible, pragmatic decisions, and say it didn't really matter that this wasn't perfect.'

In London, both the hopes of the officials and of Andersen rose as Stewart in particular tackled the problems. Stewart insists that one of the great advantages he had was the enthusiasm of Walton, an old-style civil servant approaching retirement but desperately keen to get the strategy in place, and the fact that he had control over so many facets of the operation. 'I had control over all the things that normally three or four different people would have had, and that was probably the most beneficial thing that happened,' he says. 'It's not something that normally happens in the Civil Service – usually you would be dealing with three or four different committees, and it would have been a recipe for disaster, trying to put that computer system in in such a short time-frame.'

He owed his autonomy to other factors, too. One was his personality – Stewart was almost boyish in his enthusiasm and energy, able to carry with him both his superiors and the thousands of clerks involved. He didn't mind what hours he worked or how far he travelled, just so long as he was back for Saturday's football match. His bustling energy soon gained the admiration of the Andersen staff, notably Clinton, who became a close friend, and of the officials at Caines's directorate.

The other factor was the fact that this was Scotland, which could claim to be something more than just another region. 'We could always wheel in the Scottish dimension – and we did,' says Stewart. 'You know, "Scotland is different" – the politicians do it all the time, and that helped because we could say we have to do things differently here because Scotland is different.'

His counterparts in the north-west continued to hit problems with the trade unions, still unusually militant in the area around Liverpool. In Scotland, the unions were much less militant, although still highly suspicious of the changes. 'It took a tremendous amount of talking and convincing and there was a continual dialogue with them,' recalls Stewart. 'But whereas in Merseyside they were banging off at each other, here they were very tough but pragmatic. And we got it through them and for the first time in their life they didn't act in a bureaucratic way. For instance, two trade union members would work out with my people the way forward and then that would be agreed by an overall committee we set up which met once a quarter to rubber-stamp the decisions of the smaller committees.'

The Scottish operation also differed from the north-west in the level of risks Stewart and his group were prepared to take. 'Everyone was worried at that stage: would the software work, are we actually going to have a system that we can announce on the day it needs to issue payments, or will it fall over? There were a hell of a lot of problems, but we were much more inclined to take chances,' says Stewart.

In London, too, there was much thought about the level of risk-taking. In setting the deadline, Caines was aware of the gamble he was taking, and in supporting him, Andersen was also exposed. The whole top echelon of the Department, as well as the Andersen reputation, were now committed to that date, and no one was in any doubt of the costs of failure this time round. 'The Department knew they were up against very tight deadlines, Andersen's knew they were up against very tight deadlines, and Andersen's record was on the line,' says one senior official. 'So I suppose was Caines's reputation, probably even his job. So there was a tremendous pressure on them to get users to accept anything. There was also a tremendous fear among the users that they were going to get landed, and once they accepted the system and it fell down, all the public complaint and the pressure would come down again on the users, and the technicians would say: they don't understand the system, they don't know how to work it.'

With the February 1989 deadline rapidly approaching, Ian Stewart was now working closely with the model office, picking up the lessons that came from it. Finn had built a small prototype version of the income support system, and was training people on how it would work. He took teams from the regional support groups in the north-west area and from Scotland and brought them in to test the system live. 'So they knew all the glitches, all the things you had to be wary of from day one, all the things which had been reported and been fixed, and we knew what the system was expecting. So those people, in Bolton and Edinburgh, had spent six weeks working with it, and they knew the system and the problems that people coming back from training courses would have.'

By early 1989, with the Caines deadline only weeks away, a growing number of people had been through the model-office training and were now back in the regions spreading the word that they had seen it, and it actually worked. In turn they had highlighted countless small faults in the system which the designers were able to fix. There was now a core of young, trained clerks in the social security offices waiting for the system to go live.

Changes and alterations went on right up to the final deadline. In Edinburgh, as fast as Stewart was training his teams to work on a screen, the screen intended to go into the offices altered – and went on altering. 'We were altering screens and we were altering the training system right up until the last moment,' says Stewart. It was something of a nightmare. 'You were training people that when you press this key, this is what comes up. Now if the screen comes up like something else, which is what happened in the early days, we had to reinforce the training with people going round.'

In London, concentration on the wider training programme was now the number-one priority. 'We took almost entire offices away to training centres,' says Caines. They had teams travelling around training people as well, but late on they realised they had overlooked something: they had forgotten to train the managers. Not all the managers were in favour of the strategy, and quite often they refused to have anything to do with the new system.

'The good ones came out and wanted to learn about it,' says Caines, 'and we organised last-minute courses for them. Others were terrified and locked themselves in their offices. We had to prise them out, and say, "I'm sorry, you can't go on like this." It was our fault, not theirs. We hadn't equipped them to handle all that, so it was every bit as difficult as we thought it would be.'

Local office managers objected to their staff being taken away on training courses, and to the disruption caused by installing the new system in the offices, while they had to continue running a live office, paying out benefit to a still-growing number of angry claimants.

'It was a very, very bad time,' says Caines. 'Very difficult for everybody, with the unions hopping up and down, and lots of ill-motivated information going round.'

Meanwhile, considerable interest in the strategy systems was apparent across the rest of the United Kingdom, not least in the capital. The controllers of London North and South, Ann Robinson and Ian Magee respectively, were particularly keen to exploit the opportunities offered by the new technology. For example, the strategy would enable them to move some of the most difficult work to new locations. At the same time, both were aware of the additional challenges posed by implementing such a major change in the diverse range of offices under their control. Inner city offices were hard pressed to manage even the routine business given the high turnover of staff and pressing demands of high claimant populations. Rural offices had older staff with little or no experience of computers. All offices were creaking without the systems. How could they be made to succeed with the strategy?

Robinson and Magee took a strong personal interest in the answer to that question. Robinson led a national initiative, 'Delivery of Service in the Nineties', to focus the efforts of a handful of offices on demonstrating the use of strategy systems as a springboard to improved organisation, business processes, and hence efficiency, customer service and job satisfaction. Magee supported that initiative with staff and an astute choice of offices: they took a creative, team-based approach which generated a whole series of controlled experiments with results and refinements being shared and institutionalised. As a separate strand of activity, Magee launched a communications programme in his region using internal staff and external catalysts to prepare offices and customers for the changes ahead, and to keep them informed of progress. Unlike many Departmental communications, Magee's had an attractive up-beat style and a common look and feel, so that they actively marketed the technology changes as exciting, high quality, and providing a real opportunity to effect a cultural and business change in local offices.

There were still hurdles to be leapt, but by and large the Operational Strategy was achieving at least some of its ambitious objectives. And the politicians, who had backed it warily, were ready to take some of the credit.

CHAPTER ELEVEN

IMPLEMENTATION *at* LAST

When Mrs Thatcher moved Norman Fowler to Employment and replaced him with John Moore after the election in June 1987, it was seen as a major promotion for the new Secretary of State for Social Services. For a few brief months he was seen by the political pundits as a future Prime Minister, Thatcher's chosen heir if and when she decided to step down. Even the closest of political observers failed to notice the significance of another move: John Major had done his spell at the DHSS and had been elevated to the Cabinet in the key role of chief secretary to the Treasury. From now on people would begin to pay attention to him, but that summer the man to watch was John Moore.

Moore arrived at Alexander Fleming House in the middle of the social security reforms that had been argued and debated endlessly in the election campaign. The first benefit uprating of the Fowler reforms was due in the spring of 1988, and the public and the House of Commons were much more interested in that than in the Operational Strategy, which remained very much, as it always had been as far as the public was concerned, in the background. 'In the parliamentary debates people were complaining about the family credit forms and complaining about income support and the Social Fund,' says Moore, 'not realising the enormous changes as far as the customer was concerned that would come as a result of changes in delivery on the ground.'

At first, Moore occupied himself with the policy areas, but soon had to be aware of the seriousness of the industrial unrest that was endangering his whole delivery system – as well as the complex plan for computerising it. The strikes that occurred between April and June 1987, he found, dominated the whole Department. But even allowing for that, it was difficult to get the problems and benefits of automation across to a sceptical public. 'It was very hard to explain new technology until it was up and running and working,' he says.

Once he had got his feet under the desk, Moore decided that the industrial situation had to be tackled as a priority. 'I was horrified by the ways in which pensioners and other people could have their benefits essentially stopped as a consequence of poor technology and of union domination of that technology. I wanted to take out that union dominance of the delivery of the benefits system. What I didn't immediately appreciate was how much that coincided with the views of the senior officials, who were very courageous in recognising that had to be done. And that was a fortunate coincidence.'

The fight against the unions would culminate two years later, in June 1989, with the appointment of Electronic Data Systems to run the computer centre in Livingston. Moore, as he left the Department the next day, ruefully reflected on how much had changed in that time. His political career, which had seemed so bright when he joined, was now finished, not because of the failure of the Operational Strategy to deliver, but because, like many before him, he had ended up on the wrong side of Mrs Thatcher. Much of his time in the Department had been spent trying to bring in the Operational Strategy against a backcloth of trade union attacks, delays and technical problems, but above all he had been astonished by the degree to which the strategy was still opposed at quite senior levels. In his early days, he had been astonished also by the language of the debate which the Department by that stage had become hardened to. 'You heard the argument all the time, "All you're doing is destroying long-term, good Civil Service jobs, hurting benefit recipients, reducing services, and you're bringing in all these high-paid consultants, who are just your disgusting private-sector friends",' he says.

Moore had worked in the City and industry before becoming a minister, and was more vulnerable to that type of allegation than most. But he found the senior civil servants in the Department were actually ahead of him in their rebuttal of the union claims and in their support for reducing the power of the unions. 'They handled it with enormous skill,' he says. 'All the top civil servants in the Department were committed to doing one thing which, in my view, they never got sufficient credit for: actually getting the benefit system delivered efficiently, fairly and simply.'

A civil servant, Miss Margaret Moodie, was commissioned to produce a report for the Department, which dampened everyone's spirits, although everyone must have known what it would show: the quality of service was awful. But the Moodie Report was to have considerable implications for the Department of Social Security. 'Moodie's report stated, in big headlines essentially, that the system of delivery stinks,' says Moore. Few of the benefits of computerisation were yet in effect, and the delivery system was probably at its lowest point. But Moore took the decision to publish it, warts and all. 'As a politician it was a no-win situation. The report was used by the trade unions and the Labour Party at the time to explain that the new system was never going to work, and here's how bad it is. Yet it was an attempt by us to speed up the process,' says Moore.

While waiting for the strategy to go live, Moore decided on a test of his own. He picked one of the worst areas of London, Ealing, and moved out the work processed at the local offices there to Glasgow, where unemployment was high. The new computers, once they were on-stream, should mean that benefit claims could be handled virtually anywhere in the country, and Moore wanted to investigate the possibilities of exploiting that. Parts of London had staff turnover rates of 25% and more, while in Belfast, for instance, the turnover rate was less than 2%. It worked, and soon some of the work done in London was being farmed out to high unemployment areas, with considerable success. 'We were never praised for moving jobs to those areas, as opposed to theoretically taking jobs out of London. But the ultimate aim was to try to produce better levels of service for the customers,' says Moore. The Department at that stage was trying to do something else: move from the use of the dismissive term 'benefit recipient' to the word 'customer'.

'The minute you start making people think about the

ethos of the customer with proper rights, proper interests and service and proper quality, a great deal changes,' says Moore.

Later, partly as a result of the work done by Mrs Thatcher's efficiency adviser, Sir Robin Ibbs, Moore went a stage further, and in his final months put into effect what the *Daily Telegraph* described as 'the most radical changes in the day-to-day running of the benefit system since it was established in 1948'. Under his reforms, over 80,000 civil servants would eventually find themselves working for a series of independent agencies run by newly appointed chief executives. Of these, as far as the Operational Strategy was concerned, the most important would be the Information Technology Services Agency (ITSA), which is now responsible for the day-to-day operations of the strategy systems.

What happened was this: in January 1989, Norman Clarke retired and Michael Partridge, now the permanent secretary, promoted Eric Caines into his place as Director of Social Security Operations and his Principal Establishment and Finance Officer, a Grade Two post. John Kenworthy, an ex-MoD civil servant with long experience of high-tech matters, was brought in to lead a new Information Technology Services Division, which finally gathered together all the main information technology parts of the DSS under a single command. At first he worked under Caines but, in April 1990, when ITSA was created, he was appointed as its first chief executive.

Most of the key battles had now been fought, the systems developed, exhaustively tested and tried in the model office. The big hardware orders had also been placed, not always in the way the Andersen people would have liked, but they had long learned to live with what they got. The argument over the mainframe computers had eventually gone to Cabinet and been decided on what seemed to the consultants to be purely nationalist grounds: the order went to ICL rather than IBM, but that did not worry them greatly. Similarly, the order for the terminals went to BT, but again that was not a great issue of contention: it would have created a bigger storm than anyone was prepared to face if Britain's social security system had gone to foreign companies for its computer systems. There was already enough fuss about hiring foreign-controlled consultants.

From the start, Moore was particularly impressed with Caines, who was right in the middle of his battles with the unions when he joined. 'I found him remarkable – an outstanding man, very lucid, very open, very un-civil servant-like, very direct.' He was not, he later noticed, good at presenting an idea on paper, but he made up for that in the vehemence of his arguments in committee meetings. 'Sometimes, I suppose, his critics would have said he was a bull in a china shop in the way he would seek to achieve what were in fact perfectly obvious goals.' Caines, he discovered, needed the understanding and support of his permanent secretary, and although he and Partridge were very different personalities, they were both driven by the same keen desire to make the strategy work. Partridge and Caines would never be soul-mates, but they worked well together.

While Moore was thinking about reforms, policy and structural changes – and his own political career – Caines, Andersen and their teams were running harder and harder to meet the 27 February delivery date for the LOP income support system. In Scotland, Ian Stewart found himself working through the weekends, and sometimes through the night. When a piece of software was changed in Lytham, he drove down himself to pick it up rather than wait. He was still managing the Montrose football team, but whereas two years before the team had topped the Scottish Second Division, now it was struggling in the First Division and heading for relegation again. Stewart also found himself accused, sometimes by the strategy office in London, of being 'too close' to Andersen. 'I'm quite friendly with them, I've never hidden that,' he says. 'But I was probably the toughest user, in the sense of wanting things and driving a hard bargain – but never at the expense of the project. You can be very, very tough with Andersen's, and they understand it, but you don't have to be tough to the point where you're actually going to affect the project.'

Stewart had spent a great deal of effort working up what he called his 'support teams', which he had hand-picked and given induction training to, insisting they dressed much more smartly than the ordinary social security clerk. As he trained the staff in the local offices, he often had to take up to twenty of them out of a single office for weeks on end, moving his support teams in to replace them. 'They wore badges and they were instantly recognisable. They worked any amount of hours – they were first in in the morning and last out, that was the condition of them coming in. They were the backbone of the whole thing, the way they actually performed. They were a tremendous group – there were over 100 of them – and they would do anything to make it work.'

In Lytham, the team was working equally hard. Mark Otway, the lead partner and the architect of the system, had had 'enormous doubts' that the original project could be running by February 1989. 'I never had any doubts about whether it could have been done as an exercise. But it had all been left terribly late, and I had tremendous doubts about whether there was the management will to do it.' One by one the technical problems were being solved, and Otway was happy he could handle that side of it. 'Primarily, the problems weren't technical – they were ones of scale, and maintaining consistency over a very large area and large numbers of people, and stopping people re-inventing the wheel.' The key civil servant at LOP, whom Otway worked alongside, was Kevin Caldwell. Kevin, after a broad career in the Departments of Health and of Social Security, in and out of IT, had been recruited to LOP when it moved to Lytham St Annes.

As the pressure increased at the end of 1988, his firmness of purpose and unswerving commitment matched that of Otway and his team. Their dry wit saw them over many hurdles.

At one point in particular they saw a watershed for the project: in the middle of systems-testing, with the system standing up and looking like it might process a claim or two, someone inadvertently turned on the wrong switch on the main computer. No one knew how it happened but suddenly in the middle of the night nothing worked and they were back to square one. There were about forty people there, all testing, some from Andersen and a lot of civil servants. It was 3 a.m. on a Sunday morning in January 1989. And they had a decision to make: either this was too difficult, and they would come back the next day, or they could keep on working until they found out what had happened. Following Otway and Caldwell's spirited lead, as a group they decided to keep on working. It was the key psychological point. As Otway said later, 'Once that happened, I knew it was going to work. They had decided they were not going to be beaten.'

A month before the Local Office Project went live, the Comptroller and Auditor General produced yet another report on the Operational Strategy. It was not as critical as previous reports had been: the National Audit Office, said the Comptroller, had concluded that since 1982 the Department had made 'significant progress on developing the strategy to replace existing costly clerical systems with on-line computerised systems.' There had been delays and substantial cost increases, but 'many of these were due to the complexity of the tasks undertaken.' It did, however, also have some serious criticisms: some of the delays, it said, were 'due to weaknesses in the Department's management of the strategy, particularly in the fields of planning, monitoring and resource utilisation. There were also significant weaknesses in financial planning and control.'

However, on the whole it backed the direction in which the Department was now going. The weaknesses, it concluded, had been identified and tackled – 'in some cases the action taken involved risks and expenditure which would otherwise have been avoided.'

The report also contained a section on the use of consultants where there were obvious worries about the dominance of Andersen. In 1986–7, it said, the Department had employed 150 consultants at a cost of £12.1 million. By the following year, that had risen to 235 consultants costing £22 million. The Public Accounts Committee had already expressed its own reservations about all these expensive outsiders coming in, calculating that they cost about four times their in-house equivalents. The National Audit Office found the differential had actually widened: 'The full cost including overheads of a senior executive office was about £24,000 a year while the cost of a consultant engaged on work that would be undertaken by that officer was around £115,000 a year.' This, of course, did not reflect what the consultants were actually paid: young Andersen consultants at this stage were often on salaries of around £25,000 a year, but by the time all the back-up services were taken into account, they were billed to the client at perhaps four times that. The civil servants by now understood that fully, and the resentment of the early days had waned. Indeed, the NAO report went on to point out that the Department 'stated that without consultants progress on the strategy would have been less satisfactory', and the report found that the additional costs of the consultants 'did not necessarily represent poor value for money.' Higher productivity and time saved 'might compensate for the additional cost.'

On 1 February 1989, just weeks before the project was due to go live, the Public Accounts Committee, a long-term critic of the strategy, took another look at it in the light of the NAO report, summoning Partridge, who brought with him a team of eight, including Caines. The size of the Civil Service team occasioned some ribald comments from the MPs, notably Graham Allen who, before Robert Sheldon opened the formal proceedings, chipped in with a remark to the effect that there were so many officials present he wondered if there was enough room for the public. 'I do hope that some of the social security offices out there are still functioning as a result of the attendance today,' he added.

This was perhaps the toughest grilling of all the various PAC sessions over the years, with Caines growing visibly irritated as time wore on. Partridge, however, was wonderfully placatory and disarming, as time and again he seemed to agree with the questioner – 'that is a good point, actually', he would say to an argument which he clearly thought was not at all a good one. At the beginning, Sheldon gave Partridge the opportunity for a long opening statement, which he took full advantage of in order to counter some of the Comptroller and Auditor-General's conclusions to the effect that there had been 'slippage' on all the projects, and that it had not been until 1987 that the Department had finally woken up to what was going on. 'We started with eleven projects,' explained Partridge reasonably. 'We have added ten and we have deferred four which are not now being pursued.' The strategy had changed considerably during the design stage, and it was not until 1986 that work started on bringing the whole operation together. 'In this period we had nine Acts of Parliament and 550 sets of regulations,' he added. 'These included very considerable change in the whole of social security, in income support, in the Social Fund and so on.' The strategy changed considerably, and it was only when the Department and Andersen pulled it all together that they realised how serious the slippage had been.

'At that point we saw that the additional demands, for example those created by the social security reforms, the additional demands that we had identified for control projects and also the shortages of skills which we were experiencing at that stage, and finally, industrial action which had been happening, which led to slippage on some of the projects, meant that we had to take some action.' That action had been taken promptly and effectively, he added.

One by one the committee pressed Partridge and his team (which basically meant Caines and R. Birch, the director of the regional organisation – other than the Treasury man, no one else spoke) on controlling costs. Caines at one stage could not control his gathering ire and, to Partridge's obvious discomfort, flew at the MPs. Of the seventeen projects developed over seven years, the maximum amount of slippage was four months, he pointed out, and most of them were actually being delivered on time. Where the NAO report had attacked the Department for lack of control and increased expenditure, he said, this was 'increased expenditure in certain areas with a view to delivering projects which was offset by reductions in other areas'. Caines was furious that the steps he had taken, which he believed added up to 'vigorous management', were being unfairly presented as 'being unwarranted risks that you are taking.' Caines was having none of that: 'I do think people want it all ways,' he said to the astonished MPs, who were unused to a civil servant biting back in this way.

There was a long argument over the size of the consultancy fees. The NAO report seemed to suggest that the summer 1987 estimate of £5 million for consultancy on the Lytham project had grown to £11 million when it became an emergency. 'Clearly the Department seems to have been caught in a cleft stick,' said Sir Michael Shaw. Partridge calmly explained that this was not so: every month's delay on the LOP project cost the government £7–8 million, he pointed out, and there was no time to go out to the normal tender system. 'We did a single tender. We had great difficulties with the company because they pushed up the cost to £11 million and they would not give a warranty. The outcome was we decided not to use that company, and we gave individual contracts to some people from the outside consultants and we got the work done and we actually got it done for £4.75 million. We did not actually spend the £11 million.'

Shaw was clearly impressed with that, as were the committee. But the Labour MPs on it turned to subjects of greater interest to them: the redundancies caused by the strategy, the way the Department had (mis)handled industrial relations, and the problems with the LOMP micro-computer project. There was also a long argument over what the actual costs of the project were – estimates had now reached £1.7 billion – and the savings, which had fallen as costs had risen. Towards the end, even Partridge's equanimity was starting to give, as the Labour MP Dale Campbell-Savours homed in on the cost of the consultants. He had heard that DSS staff were concerned by the size of the payments to Andersen, and by the degree of control the Department could exercise over Andersen. 'Is that correct?' he demanded of Partridge.

'No, it is not,' snapped back Partridge.

'Are Arthur Andersen acting as consultants to the

programme?' persisted Campbell-Savours.

'They are acting as consultants, they are under our control,' said Partridge defiantly. 'They work very closely in teams which have our people at their head sometimes and their people as head sometimes. They are totally under control.'

It was a sour and critical meeting, the MPs, from both sides of the House, clearly out to nail the Department while Partridge and Caines defended themselves with considerable skill (on the part of Partridge) and belligerence (from Caines). The committee made some good points, having identified from their own sources some of the problems. But in the view of Caines in particular, they did not give him enough credit for the achievements of the past year, and in particular did not as much as acknowledge that success was now only a matter of weeks away.

When the session ended at last, Caines, still seething, walked back across Parliament Square to his office, which by then was in the much more salubrious Richmond House in Whitehall. That night, Burgess and the Andersen people were joining in a celebration in the pub in Holborn to drink to the success of the project, now only days away, and Caines arrived bitterly contrasting the carping in Westminster with what he considered had been a very major achievement indeed.

The actual start-up, when it came on the due date of 27 February 1989, was something of an anticlimax. The pilot office in Bolton was originally scheduled to go on-stream a few days before Stewart's pilot office in Glasgow, but in the event Caines asked Stewart to bring the two on-stream on the same day. There were problems in Bolton, and he could not risk a failure. In neither place was it perfect, but at least it was functioning. 'It fell down a lot,' says Otway, but they had expected that, and it worked well enough for the world to see it was not another CAMELOT.

Inside the Civil Service and at Andersen there was more relief than delight. But there was no doubt among those involved as to what they had achieved. 'If I had been asked two years ago if we would be in the healthy shape we are today,

I would not have put much money on it,' wrote Alan Healey in February 1989.

In the first few weeks of March the system did what it was supposed to do. Caines, in triumphant mood, made a lightning visit to Caldwell's Local Office Project at Lytham and toured the site. After hurling his brickbats at the staff there for some many months, it was now time for some back-patting. 'It's a staggering achievement,' he told the assembled staff, 'made possible by a marvellous team working with intense dedication.' The hours put in, he added, had been 'enormous'. After all the failures, the Department had finally done it.

Andersen still had a lot of work to do, however, before its job was finished. There was six months to learn the lessons from the pilot project before starting national roll-out in October 1989, and it was an invaluable time. Again, as so often in the past, real problems generated by real people in the real world were found to be different from anything imagined in the laboratories. Andersen also discovered that no matter how carefully it had planned, crucial pieces were still missed out. 'Part of the training we missed was making sure people knew what happened after the information went away from their screen,' says Philippa Reid. 'Consequently, people didn't trust the computer and they'd come in the next day and find each of those cases and say, "Oh, yes, they've done it", and then they'd say, "Oh, that figure doesn't look right", and they'd go and work it out manually to see whether the computer had got it right. Of course, it had, and nine times out of ten it was they who were doing it wrong, and in the meantime you wasted a huge amount of time while they worked it out for themselves.'

Through the summer and autumn of 1989, Andersen and the Department devised intensive three-day training sessions to train the managers themselves in what to expect from the system, and what it would do for their workload. Andersen were also carrying out a study on the whole implementation process. By June, there were enough offices on the system for them to examine how it was working, and they carried out a detailed study. Were they going about it in the right way?

The system seemed to be holding up.

In September 1989, Caines called a conference in St Albans to review progress so far. Philippa Reid, who had spent the summer working on a report, had a miscarriage and wasn't there. Caines was at his bluntest at a meeting which few enjoyed. The technical side of the Operational Strategy, he said, was now in place and working, and all the hopes for that had been vindicated. The five major projects which they had concentrated on had all gone live and, once the glitches had been ironed out, were standing up to the test of actual use. But where the whole strategy was falling down was on the user side, which Caines had only recently taken responsibility for. Stewart, who made a presentation about his success in Scotland, supported him, even though he was a user. Others were much more sceptical, and those who were there – the Andersen people present played little part – remember a harsh, unpleasant meeting, with no sense of euphoria.

Nonetheless, the Operational Strategy was up and running. Over the next eighteen months it would continue to go through problems, but on the whole the conversion of the clerks at the desks of the local offices went remarkably well, especially through 1990 and 1991, when office after office went live with virtually no interruptions to service. 'They took to it like ducks to water,' says John Kenworthy. 'Demands for a better service, a cleverer service and a quicker service came through very quickly.'

Caines might have complained about the reaction of the user side at the beginning, but by 1990, when roll-out was running at seven offices a week, that had improved sharply. 'There was a little bit of a shock to people who had been isolated on this huge project for a long time when it went live,' says Kenworthy. 'They had built this enormous structure and now it was about to move, and they hated it when the user started criticising it. They had expected too much of it at the beginning. But if you look at the total time scale between pilot and July 1991 when the last office went live, it has been a remarkable success. The smoothness with which roll-out went from the first fifty offices by the autumn of 1989, when we had a pause to assess what we were doing, and then the other 450 offices, was astonishing.'

POSTSCRIPT

In the event, the report from the House of Commons Public Accounts Committee was sceptical of the Department, concluding, to the irritation of the senior officials, that costs had not been kept fully under control at all stages. Both Partridge and Caines had tried to drive home what for them was the central argument on the costs front: yes, the costs of the Operational Strategy would indeed rise from £700 million to £1.8 billion by the year 2000, but that did not constitute a failure of control. What had happened, they argued, was that there had been a 'proper' expansion of the number of projects once the Department (and ministers) had grasped the full possibilities of extending computerisation. They tried to outline their thoughts on what they described as 'getting better value for money across a much wider area', but this point never quite got through to the MPs. Partridge in particular would later feel that the committee had not fully appreciated the Department's need to invest up-front, 'to show improvements in quality of service and savings over time, rather than simply looking at a given sum of money and seeing whether more than that had been spent'.

The fact of the matter was that, in the dozen years since Norman Clarke first put pen to paper, the project had altered out of all recognition. The strategy turned out not to be a single project but a whole series of them, linked through the Departmental Central Index, and even now not yet all completed. When finally finished in the mid-1990s, the cost will add up to an investment of nearly £1.8 billion (not allowing for inflation), which is roughly three times the cost originally estimated. That, however, has to be balanced against the benefits which, the Department would argue, were much more than three times greater, many of them not measurable in hard money terms.

The need for mechanisation in the social security system had been identified more than twenty years earlier. But what had not been foreseen were the new ways the systems would be used once computerisation was in place. In the first few years, the Central Index was used so much that its capacity had to be doubled – and then doubled again. And as the supply system improved, so demand went on rising. 'People have found themselves with a tool they are using in ways we couldn't have expected,' says John Kenworthy.

But now at least the system could cope. The speed-up in the process of applications in offices, which themselves had been greatly upgraded, was visible to all. The computer systems had done what they set out to do, and taken away much of the drudgery of manual processing, got rid of the piles of paper, given staff increased responsibility and job satisfaction, and substantially reduced the error rate. Now benefits, such as child support, could be plugged into the system without straining it.

That was the good side. The bad side was that the savings were rather less than planned, due to some extent to the increase in benefits over the period, but also to the higher costs. Nonetheless, at the end of the day the Department could point with some satisfaction to its latest estimate that savings would rise to £150 million a year by 1995 – a useful bonus on top of the improved service.

So at the end of the day, was the whole story a success? Undoubtedly senior officials in the Department and ministers – and certainly those concerned at Andersen – think so. The PAC may have its doubts, but it has to be said that in pure management and business terms the strategy worked and achieved most or all – in some cases much more – that it set out to do. More important in retrospect, however, are the changes it has brought about in the management approach of the Department. When Clarke began his work, with CAMELOT falling apart, morale had been low and sinking lower. Andersen, in the early days, had been struck by the lack of confidence in tackling new projects and getting straightforward things done. But the Operational Strategy had restored the Department's faith in itself, persuading it that it could plan and deliver change successfully on a large scale and to a tight timetable. It also gave its top managers the confidence to embark on huge changes in the Department's own structure and organisation, making use of the new technology that was transforming the working lives of its big battalions of staff in the front line, who were dealing day to day with the public. It is difficult to explain that to the PAC, and impossible to quantify it in cash terms.

As events were to turn out, the system was in place only in the nick of time. Even before LOP was rolling out into the last local office (ahead of schedule) in the summer of 1991, the Department under Michael Partridge was planning the largest shake-up it had known in its forty-year history. Hard on the heels of the 1988 division of the DHSS into the two departments in which it logically belonged – Health and Social Security, the two having only come together twenty years earlier to create a power-base for Richard Crossman – the new DSS was planning to take advantage of the Next Steps initiative launched by Mrs Thatcher as Prime Minister following a report bearing that title from her efficiency adviser, Sir Robin Ibbs. The aim was to put all operational activities of central government into agencies, headed by a chief executive and run on more business-like lines. Each agency would have clear aims and objectives, laid down by ministers, and greater freedom from traditional Civil Service central constraints on how those aims and objectives were to be delivered.

Next Steps was not greeted with enthusiasm everywhere in Whitehall, but in the DSS, which had been developing systems objectives, performance measures and delegated management for some fifteen years, Partridge took advantage of it to turn what had been a geographically based department, with its powerful barons in Newcastle, Reading and elsewhere, into a functional one. Now, instead of local and central offices administering a mixture of benefits, contributions and information technology, there was to be a clear division into separate businesses. Separate agencies were set up, each with its own chief executive, some from outside the Civil Service. The areas of contributions, information technology (run by Kenworthy), most social security benefits (whether central or local), employment services (including unemployment benefit) and resettlement services would have their own agencies, all of them set up and working by 1992, by which stage 97% of the Department's

80,000 staff would be working in them. Only a hard core of 1200 people remained at headquarters. Two more agencies would later be created to handle war pensioners' affairs jointly with the Ministry of Defence, and the new child maintenance arrangements legislated for in 1991.

In the process of all this, working practices and traditions changed radically, with whole layers of management stripped out, and several hundred people in middle and senior management given early retirement. It is doubtful whether these changes could have been made or carried through so quickly and effectively if it had not been for the Operational Strategy. Nor might top management and ministers have had the confidence to undertake this if they had not been riding the wave of success of introducing that strategy.

And the process went even further. One key feature of the Next Steps reforms was to focus on the customer rather than on what it suited the bureaucracy to give him. That built on the vision that lay at the heart of the Operational Strategy, the 'whole person' concept, bringing all the Department's information and procedures together through new technology to serve the customer at the point of contact with the Department. Now, with the right system in place, the 'whole person' concept could be developed through new generations of terminals and other hardware. 'Once you have the network, and the main systems backing it up,' says John Kenworthy, 'you can do what you want. There is for instance nothing to stop you putting terminals anywhere in the high street. We will eventually move to new terminals which will have the ability to talk directly to the individual, and we can give the customer direct access. It's dicey for the data base right now, but there is no reason why they shouldn't make an inquiry. All these things are technically on the table now.'

There are still Andersen people in the Department, and will be for many years, as the systems continue to develop. But the Department has generated a considerable number of skilled and talented people in its own right. 'Skill transfer has been vitally important,' says Kenworthy. 'I always insist on it, and Andersen have willingly given it, and by their own admission have learned much from working with my people too. The running of the systems now is very much a matter for my agency, and that is very important.' At the height of the project, 2000 people, civil servants and consultants, were working together in close-knit, cross-functional teams, with the Department's staff picking up the skills and – more importantly – the best of both cultures coming to the fore.

The Department had discovered that a fifth of all customers first come into contact with the social security system in hospitals, and Kenworthy was now planning to install terminals in the reception areas supplying child benefit, income support, unemployment pay and so on. He saw no reason why he should not run all the services into unemployment offices too. 'The idea is one-stop shopping – the whole person concept is very much alive.'

The concept of the customer as king – or at least as an individual who mattered – was taken further in July 1991, when John Major published details of his Citizen's Charter, which he indicated would be the central plank of Tory policy while he was Prime Minister. In the light of events since, some of it would have a hollow ring, but at the time it struck a chord with what the Department was trying to achieve with the Operational Strategy. It was designed, as Major wrote in his foreword, 'to make public services answer better to the wishes of their users'. Although it would be greeted with a certain amount of scepticism, a number of the objectives would find widespread support from those who had worked on the DSS's Operational Strategy. The government, said the White Paper, was determined 'to drive reforms further into the core of the public services', and to raise quality, 'secure better value and extend accountability'. There was a special section devoted to the Social Securities Benefits Agency, set up the previous April to improve further the delivery of social security benefits, which spelt out the way in which the Prime Minister's thoughts on the future were developing. There would, he said, be a 'customer charter', which would publish national and regional targets for all the main benefit services. 'Information on local office performance will be displayed prominently in every office.'

In one sense, the charter could be interpreted as a recognition by John Major that nothing much had changed, and that discontent was still high. But there was another, and fairer, way of looking at it. Without the success of the strategy, Major would not even have been able to make the promises he did – or boast that the accuracy of unemployment benefit payment was 95.2% against a target of 95%. Retirement pension claims, which took thirty-one days to be cleared in 1985–6, had come down to twenty-one days in 1989–90, and fell again the following year; 95% of income support claims were being cleared in four days.

For its part, the DSS responded quickly and enthusiastically enough, with the Benefits Agency and the Contributions Agency being among the first to produce Citizen's Charters and to publish national and local targets and independent surveys of customer opinion on the services provided. On the other hand, keener observers felt that, with the completion of the system, there were signs that the momentum of reform was slackening. Officials who had worked flat out to get the system in place now seemed to feel that their job was done, and someone else could carry on where they had left off. Those who had felt that a permanent cultural change had been effected began to have doubts. Those who had once admired the determination of officials such as Otton, Partridge, Clarke and Caines to push through the changes sensed a lack of innovative thinking. There was no longer a Clarke-style think-tank, looking at the way benefits would develop in the next century, nor was there any overriding target, which the strategy had provided for all those years. Ministers and officials would argue that they don't need one, that the strategy was a once-in-a-century operation, and that the changes, the structure and the technology in place now will last for twenty years. They also argue that all the reforms described in this book are now coming together, in a new style of departmental management that is more genuinely strategic at the top and includes more genuine delegation of responsibilities and resources down through agency chief executives to local managers.

On the other hand, there may have been opportunities

missed for capitalising on the considerable breakthroughs that were in place by 1990. Andersen at one stage organised a study of much more automated and streamlined methods of paying benefits – using 'smart' cards, for instance, which would contain all the information needed for a claimant to draw out cash from any automatic teller machine in a bank or building society. The Department, which in its 1989 mood was enthusiastic, had changed its mind two years later, and the study was cancelled.

These may be no more than minor quibbles set against a solid block of accomplishment, but even some of those most deeply involved – and now out of it – see a danger that an old, all-too-familiar trend may be re-emerging. In the early 1960s, the Department made tremendous strides in automation and delivery of very complex benefits. Then it slowly ossified, until the early 1980s, when it needed a huge jolt to get it moving again. Is it in danger of ossifying again? 'Will there be a group of civil servants and politicians who are prepared to go and address major issues of planning and delivering new benefits seriously, as opposed to tinkering with them?' asks one of the Andersen men.

Most important of all, will the culture changes, nursed into being at such effort, last? It is just possible that a decade from now, the Operational Strategy will be seen, not as the beginning of a continuing change, but as an imaginative, courageous but one-off shift that brought the DSS into the 1990s, but not into the twenty-first century, which is when it will need to work at its best. The systems are in place, the teams have been trained and are eager enough to move forward, and the demand from the customer is present. What may however be lacking is the political will. Does John Major really mean it when he says he wants to carry the reforms envisioned in his Citizen's Charter 'into new territory'? If he doesn't, he will be missing a wonderful opportunity to capitalise on the extraordinary efforts, imagination and skills of a group of dedicated people who made the DSS's Operational Strategy happen in the 1980s.

The Department robustly rejects the doubts and criticisms, and offers up its own more optimistic picture of the future. As it sees it, the story is by no means finished, and in many ways may just have begun. The implications of the Operational Strategy, of its new agencies and of the Citizen's Charter, are much greater than has commonly been perceived up to now. Ministers and the senior management of the Department are now looking strategically at the whole shape of benefits and contributions: are they best suited to customers, and to the delivery of good service? Or are they a set of legislative pigeon-holes into which customers have to be fitted? Other questions too, they say, are being asked – and tackled.

Are the delivery systems and procedures really geared to customers, or to the interests and convenience of those giving the service? Could the information technology revolution be taken much further, with customers not having to go to any office at all, and with all transactions conducted by computer links and credit transfer? Could the DSS partnership with the private sector be developed, not just with existing plans for extending market testing and contracting out, but to the point where customers have a real choice, instead of the present public-service monopoly?

These questions are certainly being asked. Whether or not they are successfully tackled is of vital importance to millions of people. But that is the subject of another book.

INDEX

INDEX